1,000,000 Books

are available to read at

---◆---

www.ForgottenBooks.com

---◆---

Read online
Download PDF
Purchase in p:

ISBN 978-1-334-04637-7
PIBN 10559566

1 MONTH OF
FREE
READING

at

www.ForgottenBooks.com

By purchasing this book you are eligible for one month membership to ForgottenBooks.com, giving you unlimited access to our entire collection of over 1,000,000 titles via our web site and mobile apps.

To claim your free month visit:
www.forgottenbooks.com/free559566

English
Français
Deutsche
Italiano
Español
Português

www.forgottenbooks.com

Mythology Photography **Fiction**
Fishing Christianity **Art** Cooking
Essays Buddhism Freemasonry
Medicine **Biology** Music **Ancient
Egypt** Evolution Carpentry Physics
Dance Geology **Mathematics** Fitness
Shakespeare **Folklore** Yoga Marketing
Confidence Immortality Biographies
Poetry **Psychology** Witchcraft
Electronics Chemistry History **Law**
Accounting **Philosophy** Anthropology
Alchemy Drama Quantum Mechanics
Atheism Sexual Health **Ancient History**
Entrepreneurship Languages Sport
Paleontology Needlework Islam
Metaphysics Investment Archaeology
Parenting Statistics Criminology
Motivational

MICHEL SAINT-DENIS

MICHEL SAINT-DENIS

THEATRE

THE REDISCOVERY

OF STYLE

Introduction by

SIR LAURENCE OLIVIER

THEATRE ARTS BOOKS

NEW YORK

1960

Published in 1960
Reprinted 1965

Theatre Arts Books
333 Sixth Avenue
New York 14, N.Y.
Printed in Great Britain

To
GEORGE DEVINE
AND
GLEN BYAM SHAW
MY FRIENDS
IN MEMORY OF OUR COMMON WORK

CONTENTS

PLATES

INTRODUCTION

by

SIR LAURENCE OLIVIER

'I FIND IT GOOD, but a little . . . *short*,' were the first words
spoken to me by Michel Saint-Denis. I had just played Romeo
for the first time and about that no more need be said; I merely
quote words which to me are memorable because they have
always represented for me the two most remarkable qualities of
this unique 'homme de théâtre'; a rare insight and a shrewd
choice of words in their language which many of his English
colleagues must have envied.

I did not myself come under his direct influence until 1938.
By this time his initial artistic success in this country had been
established, and his influence acknowledged through his presentation of the Compagnie des Quinze and his *Noah* of John
Gielgud and with his charge of the London Theatre Studio. I
myself was delighted to be on the council of this and so won my
introduction to the vivid lines of his theatrical imagination, and
the peculiarly spell-binding qualities of his teaching. I do not
think that his influences in these respects were universal, but I
do think that those once fascinated by him remained so. Rightly
or wrongly he excited obedience, and in my case, as with many
another, with never a flick of rebelliousness. You either believed
in the man or you didn't, but something told you instinctively

that you had better do so if you were to get any good out of him.
This resulted in a kind of enslavement which, though not at all
disagreeable, was apt to make you feel like a donkey enticed by
a different carrot at every milepost along a road that kept re-
appearing ahead of you just when you thought you had come to
the end of it. There seemed to be no limit to the amount of new
demands which he made upon his actors in things to do with
characterisation, expression or dimension. My first real work
with him, as I have said, was in 1938; this was in an ill-fated
production of *Macbeth* at the Old Vic. The play was living up
to its fateful reputation; Lilian Bayliss died the day of the first
night, and this had already had to be postponed owing to the
intricate nature of the production which no stage staff could
have learnt in the customary time allotted, and the temporary
failure of my vocal cords to find any vibratory meeting place.
This failure, and that of a later production of *Twelfth Night* promoted the thought that Shakespeare was not his forte, and that
the true conductorship of it was not to be found in the Frenchman's cunning (see p. 24. 'Shakespeare is not a classic'). Looking
back on it after many years and many talks with him on various
occasions, it has occurred to me that his sense of character
building might have been too precise for the sometimes way-
ward tricks exacted by the great magic wand. What would a
Coriolanus do if required to speak, 'The Moon of Rome, chaste
as the icicle that's curded by the frost from purest snow and
hangs on Dian's Temple; dear Valeria' – in character!

However, the chief good and market of his theory has ever
been to find the truth *through* the verse, and as time has worn on,
his direction has laid more emphasis upon a conception continent
within the form, and less upon a consistency of character line
which could disturb it.

Howbeit, there was something to me about his theory that provoked an interest and a fascination which no charge of failure could have diminished, and it was with the freshest kind of faith that I again placed myself entirely happily in his hands for his production of *Oedipus*. I have never been an actor who cares much for being extemporised upon by a director, rather fancying that I could do that all right for myself, but I would always respect a plan, and Michel's plans were things of rare precision. If required to move exactly two feet three inches in any direction on a certain word I found it more amusing and stimulating to rest confident that the reason and the truth in the direction would be apparent in two or three days' time, than to question it then and there.

His *Oedipus* was a success, and there is no question that Michel's successes have always been dazzling in their brilliance. His *Three Sisters* for John Gielgud, though it only ran six weeks or so in 1939, has been held to be the definitive production of this play in our profession ever since, and even its recent presentation by the Moscow Arts did nothing to obliterate its memory or in any way surpass it, and this without the unquestionable benefit of having a permanent company under his hands.

Apart from his creative genius, he is a man of extraordinary administrative capabilities. Of his theory and practice in the Arts and Sciences of theatre training, no doubt much will be learnt in the following pages. I will content myself with saying that the breaking up of the Old Vic Theatre School, the Young Vic and the Old Vic Theatre Centre led by those wonderful men Glen Byam Shaw and George Devine under the inspiration and supervision of Michel Saint Denis, was a great and dire tragedy in the life of our theatre.

Our history boasts an unfortunate amount of crass mistakes which it is proud to throw up to reflect our glories, and the decision of the powers that were at the time, that this work was dispensable, was as unimaginatively misguided as Prinny turning his back on Nelson in public, and no doubt will be passed off with the customary apologetic smirk.

Great as his loss has been to the Old Vic Theatre Centre as it was dreamed of in the years ago, and to those of us who dreamed of it, the time has not been lost to himself or to the enterprises on which he has since shed the light of his understanding, and now this seems to be reflected by a manifold and abundant fruition. Strasbourg, the Juilliard School of Music, the Lincoln Theatre Centre and the Inspectorship General of the Theatre in France; all these, and perhaps more, are now to be blest by the marriage of his intuition with his experience. Perhaps too, we early friends of those 'best years of his maturity' can indulge in speculative hopes of again being cast under the rich eloquence of his artistic apprehension, enjoying again the rough blanket of his friendship with that pineapple astringency of personality.

PREFACE

I GAVE the five informal lectures which comprise this book soon after my arrival in the United States in March 1958. It was my first visit.

I had been invited to America as 'consultant' to the Juilliard School of Music following upon the completion of an enquiry about theatre training conducted in Europe and the United States by the Rockefeller Foundation.

The Lincoln Centre for the Performing Arts was being planned, and the Juilliard School of Music had agreed to establish a progressive institution for advanced training in theatre art.

I had met representatives of the Rockefeller Foundation very briefly in Strasbourg where I was working at the time, and preliminary conversations in New York led me to understand that I had been called upon as a result of my familiarity with the classical theatre both in England and France, combined with a contemporary approach both to education and training for the stage.

My former acquaintanceship with members of the American Group Theatre and the information I had gathered particularly from reading Harold Clurman's *The Fervent Years* had prepared me to appreciate in America the development of a realistic tradition more or less based upon Stanislavski's example and teachings. I found that the American theatre, not only by 'method', but in basic outlook and, so to speak, by constitution, was realistic. Any evolution, whether in subject-matter or style. the need for which was being expressed by several dramatists, directors, and critics, would have to start from the deeply ploughed field of realism in its different aspects.

During my first fortnight in New York, in the atmosphere of the Broadway and off-Broadway theatres, I remodelled my lectures. It seemed to me essential that my European attitude, formed out of a fusion between traditional 'theatricality' and the ever-growing influence of European realism, should be presented within the framework of the young but already ingrained American realistic tradition. In my four lectures given to the American Shakespeare Festival and Academy at the Plymouth theatre, New York, I developed this idea under the general title of *Classical Theatre and Modern Realism*. The Theodore Spencer lecture, which I gave in Harvard University, is devoted to the French theatre, classical and modern, in which theatrical evolution is greatly nourished by tradition. I hope that it will complete the purpose of this book.

I am glad to express here my deep gratitude to my friend John Allen, who brought his kind understanding to the revision of my text, which was spoken in 'corrupted' English. My thanks are also addressed to Marion Watson and Barbara Goodwin, who helped me during the preparation of these lectures; to Jack Landau who with John Houseman was my host at the American Shakespeare Festival and Academy in New York; and Robert Chapman my host at Harvard.

NEW YORK   MICHEL SAINT-DENIS

PART ONE

THE CLASSICAL

THEATRE

THE CLASSICAL

FRENCH TRADITION

CONTRADICTIONS AND

CONTRIBUTIONS

LADIES AND GENTLEMEN. Knowing the names of the poets, the scholars, and of the men of the theatre who have spoken here before me, I realise the great honour you have paid me in inviting me to speak for the first time in Harvard in memory of a man whom you cherish for all that he did for letters, the arts, and the theatre of your country.

I shall try to tell you simply of my experience in the theatre. Next year I shall have been in the theatre for forty years. I began in 1919, just after the First World War; I've only been interrupted once in that work, and that was by the Second World War. I mention the two wars because they have been of great importance to me: in tragic circumstances, they have connected me with other men. It is thanks to these wars, perhaps, that I have avoided being confined to the world of the theatre, the atmosphere of which is sometimes rarefied and artificial.

If I have partly escaped the theatre, I am glad also that I have partly escaped my French nationality. I know that that is a dangerous attitude to take ... I've spent twenty years of my life, the best years of my maturity, living in England and working with the English theatre. What I probably mean is that I feel in

[17]

a position to understand my own country better through having been so long away from it.

Now I've got to make a final preliminary confession. I've always belonged to non-conforming organisations. I began in Paris with Jacques Copeau at the Théâtre du Vieux Colombier, the beginnings of which were not easy. When I became myself the head of a company – it was the Compagnie des Quinze – I played a repertory of plays of the sort that were not fashionable in Paris at the time. I have established three different schools of the theatre and I have always encouraged my students to join me in discovering new ways of stimulating their creative imagination and an approach to their interpretative work which could give reality to style. I have never directed a play I did not like. I have never directed 'boulevard' or 'West-end' plays. I must say that I have not often been asked to. The theatre is divided into very definite families.

Finally, in spite of appearances – for I was a part of the Old Vic for six years – I've always been much more concerned with the modern than with the classical theatre. I could say of my work that during these forty years it has been, and still is, an experiment directed towards the discovery of all the means by which reality can be given to fiction on the stage.

I have now finished what is called an 'introduction': and you know the ghosts and shadows with which I am accompanied in my first contact with Broadway, with the American theatre, with America and Americans.

I am French: there's no doubt about it. I leave it to you to appreciate the normal consequences of being French. People have many different ideas about it. But from a theatrical point of view these consequences are precise, even if they are not always very well known.

I discovered, once I was outside France, that the English, and, I believe, the American people mean by 'classics' all the great dramatists of the past, including those of the recent past; so that in your terms, Ibsen and Chekhov are 'classics'; and I believe it is true that you even refer to Bernard Shaw and Eugene O'Neill as classics.

With us it is not at all the same. For a Frenchman classicism is a spirit, a philosophy, a form. In fact if you speak to a French purist, and we have a few, you will find him asserting that only one aspect of his own civilisation is worthy to be described as 'classical': the period that was born from Rabelais and Montaigne in the pre-classical age, and went on to blossom with Descartes and Pascal in philosophy, Poussin in painting, Lulli in music, Corneille, Racine, and Molière in drama. Here we are at the summit of the true French classical period. The sixteenth century is excluded: the style of Louis XIII, easily remembered as that of *The Three Musketeers*, is too heavy, too fleshy. The style of Louis XV is too mannered, too frail. No, Louis XIV, 'le Roi Soleil', the king who modestly chose the sun as symbol of his glory, stands in the centre of the classical age. Regnard and Marivaux, dramatists of the eighteenth century, will be admitted into it by extension, but the door will be shut in front of Beaumarchais, already corrupted in spirit and form.

It is by a sort of considered need for affiliation that French classicism has recognised its ancestors: the classical period of Greece (Aeschylus, Sophocles, Euripides); Roman comedy (Terence and Plautus); and even the comedians of the Commedia dell' Arte. But those buffoons from the south needed Molière, to give their work shape.

Such is really the nature of the milk by which every French

child is nurtured at school and in life. He is educated in the Humanities according to the classical disciplines. The same discipline survives in Universities, in Academies, in literature, in the arts, and in the theatre. To this classical tradition we revert continually; very often to oppose it. But it remains a basic measure, the standard of quality. It is embodied most tellingly in Molière: La Comédie Française is called 'La Maison de Molière; The Home of Molière'; it is supposed to have transmitted up till today the traditions of Molière's company. You can see it symbolised by the very armchair in which Molière died while playing *Le Malade Imaginaire*. Very often this chair travels with the company. When they went to Moscow they took it with them; they were not playing *Le Malade Imaginaire*; just as a sign of Molière; complete Molière in wood. And the French National Conservatoire, the official school of dramatic art, is a place where some great actors 'de la maison' teach; and they take seriously their function, which is to pass on to the young the traditional way of playing classical texts and consequently the meaning of the classical style.

Now it is very easy to laugh at such a conservative spirit, especially if one is completely foreign to it. We have suffered from this spirit enough, we French, to see the merit in laughing also. It is evident that one cannot transmit a literal tradition from generation to generation and keep it alive. Nobody with any intelligence ever thought that that was possible.

Fortunately we have the texts, which should lead us to the spirit. To be classical is to be impersonal and objective. It does not mean to avoid detailed characterisation, but to create characters which instead of being detailed, with a subjective, realistic psychology, remain objective. It tends to create types which in a balanced civilisation will be generally recognised.

The language, usually eloquent, is loaded with human matter. Born of an aristocratic society, this form of art is aristocratic in expression: vigorous and heroic in Corneille, tender and passionate in Racine, more popular in Molière. And in the tragedy of Racine and Corneille, or in high comedy, like Molière's *Misanthrope*, the text is written in verses of twelve feet, usually divided in the middle, with a rhyme at the end. Nothing less. You can imagine that actors do not find this style easy to tackle, though at the same time it has flexibility. Needless to say that to discover this flexibility and to preserve the form of the verse requires considerable art. Similarly the prose, the great prose of Molière, is also calculated, numbered prose, so written that it tends towards prosody.

Now you may find such a style so exacting that it becomes boring. It is the contrary of naturalism: probably the most isolated, but at the same time the highest form of theatre in the whole of Western Europe. It is also, as I know from experience, the most remote from the Anglo-Saxon world. I have had the opportunity of reading some Molière to audiences in London, and they were often pleased; but when I tried Racine, even those English people most familiar with French culture and ready to appreciate a certain form of classicism, could not 'take' him. And I had chosen *Phèdre*, which is rich in dramatic events and tension; but even so they could not accept it – 'talk, talk, talk,' they said, 'it's too rhetorical, too formal, at the expense of action, of life, of reality.'

One must say that it is becoming increasingly difficult for us to find actors capable of playing in the style of Corneille and Racine because the kind of classical measure and discipline it requires goes further and further away from modern life.

I have always worked, I've said, with non-conforming people, who, starting afresh from the texts, have re-created the tradition, very often against the rulings of the Comédie Française.

First of all, in 1913, I saw Charles Dullin play Molière's *L'Avare*. I saw it again in 1922. Dullin was still playing *L'Avare* when he died, a few years ago. He brought to the rôle, not realism, but a reality which restored the vitality that a conventional respect for tradition had destroyed.

In 1922 I heard some public readings by Copeau. He was an extraordinary reader. A lot of his influence came through his readings. He read *Bérénice*. Do you know *Bérénice*? It is the most motionless of Racine's plays. Its subject comes from Tacitus and is expressed by 'invitus invitam dimisit' – 'in spite of himself, in spite of herself, they parted'. That's all. No other matter: solely the movement of lovers quitting and lovers coming back. It concerns four people with their servants. Copeau always said that such plays, instead of being played in the open air, in big places, should be performed in a small auditorium made of wood, where the sound of the text would have the quality of chamber music; the tone of the voices, the variety of pitch, the positions of the characters, their extreme economy of movement and gesture, all must be arranged so that nothing should trouble the air but beautiful sound and rare motion. Racine requires near immobility; the whole of the action being an inner one, it has to be expressed outwardly with the utmost sensitivity. You see that it is all very refined.

In 1920 Copeau gave a production of *Les Fourberies de Scapin* by Molière. Set on a bare platform, ruthlessly lit like a boxing ring, it recaptured the spirit of the Commedia dell' Arte without any laborious imitation of the past.

In 1923 *Le Misanthrope* was directed and acted by Copeau. I was the stage-manager. It was performed in front of a tapestry, with four armchairs and a stool in the middle of the stage. A few hats, a few sticks, and a few swords: no other properties. Two letters, I think. When Copeau, who played Alceste, came on to the stage before the show, I used to be told every night that the armchairs, set on a very beautiful carpet, so that I could not mark the positions, were wrongly set. And I assure you that they were always exactly in position. Copeau was in the mood of Alceste for about two hours before the curtain rose – such was the 'reality' needed to animate the great style of the play.

In 1935 there was Jouvet in *L'École des Femmes*, playing Arnolphe in the famous Bérard set.

In 1949 there was Jouvet in *Tartuffe* with scenery by Braque.

In 1952 a newcomer, Jean Vilar, was acclaimed as an innovator because of his interpretation of Corneille's *Le Cid*, a tragedy in the rhetorical and lyrical style. Gérard Philipe was Rodrigue.

In 1954 I saw Vilar's *Don Juan* by Molière, at the Avignon Festival, a magnificent performance. At the end I was standing on my feet and shouting: the relationship between Don Juan and Sganarelle appeared in a new light, much more illuminating than at the Comédie Française. Don Juan was more of an atheist than a seducer; and Sganarelle was the common man serving the aristocratic unbeliever and watching with terror and admiration his master's challenge to God.

All these productions have had a profound influence on the contemporary theatre in France and abroad. I've mentioned them because they are milestones: the 'classics' have made an important contribution to the modern style. You yourselves have seen here Jean-Louis Barrault in *Les Fausses Confidences* by Marivaux. Not very long ago Moscow applauded La Comédie

Française in *Le Bourgeois Gentilhomme* by Molière, and Jean Vilar in *Le Triomphe de L'Amour* by Marivaux and also in Molière's *Don Juan* and *Marie Stuart* by Victor Hugo. I went to Moscow in June 1957 and when I asked the Russians what they liked best from the repertories of Brecht, the Comédie Française, and Jean Vilar, they answered without any hesitation, Marivaux. I asked them why. They said, 'Because of its style: it's something we cannot do ourselves. From Brecht we have nothing to learn, we have done it before him. But the kind of diction and physical elegance required by the French plays of the eighteenth century, that's what we need.'

Why are the Russians so sensitive to that kind of art? Why do they want to learn from it? Why on their own stages do they regularly act Molière and Shakespeare?

According to French rule, custom, and vocabulary, Shakespeare is not a classic. Everybody knows that up to the time of Victòr Hugo in the middle of the nineteenth century, the French considered Shakespeare a barbarian. His plays were excessive, without discipline, without taste; he was a man without balance, mixing comedy with tragedy, which according to the rules of the classicist you cannot do: each style must be kept separate. Then the French Romantics, Hugo and Musset, tried to imitate Shakespeare, but in most of their plays they failed; they retained only superficial likenesses: they never got to the heart of Shakespearian reality, which is something of flesh, of passion, of blood, which gives body to the spirit; and all expressed in a language which is less restricted than the French, but which is all the same perfectly measured, with its own subtle laws. Until about 1910 the French considered Shakespeare in the light of French romanticism and the literary battle between the classics and the romantics. Shakespeare was a romantic and Racine was a classic, the representative of the truly French tradition. During this intermediate period, translators and adaptors tended to simplify Shakespeare, to bring order to his plays, to 'classicize' them.

Since 1910 the influence of Shakespeare has prevailed in France to an extent I doubt whether you realise. The naturalists of whom the first was André Antoine, got hold of Shakespeare and produced, for instance, *King Lear* with so much emphasis upon the storm as to drown the words. A little later Firmin Gémier gave popular shows of a spectacular kind in a circus. When the anti-naturalistic school triumphed with Copeau – that was from 1913 onwards – not only Shakespeare but many of the Elizabethan dramatists began to be performed, and on the architectural or formal stages of Copeau, Dullin and Pitoëff, there were to be seen the plays of Webster, Tourneur, Ford and Thomas Kyd, alternating with Ben Jonson, Thomas Heywood, and Beaumont and Fletcher. The Théâtre du Vieux Colombier opened in 1913 with *A Woman Killed with Kindness* by Heywood. It closed its first season in 1914 with the great success of *Twelfth Night,* and it reopened in 1920 with *The Winter's Tale.* Don't you find these facts significant? This new development in France is in line with the influence of Freud and of surrealism. New translations, together with less constrained productions, cultivate the contrasts in Shakespeare's style, give expression to his violence, mark the changes in tone and in location. But up to the war these productions remained the privilege of cultured people belonging to the 'avant-garde'. Shakespeare and the Elizabethan dramatists were performed because they combined 'theatricality' with deep meaning.

When in 1934 I went to work in the London theatre, I found the popular Shakespeare of the English. I arrived at a moment when the reforms brought about by William Poel and Granville Barker had placed Shakespeare again in a suitable architecture, with a minimum of scenery, so that the original composition of the plays could be respected without undue pauses between the scenes.

It was also the time when interpretation and production were being influenced by modern realism, with the effect that human truth had come to be considered more important than the famous 'music of words': the result was that rhetoric or lyrical delirium had to go. It was then that I understood, more clearly than I have ever done with Racine and Corneille, how poetry is better able to express reality than the so-called 'realistic' language of everyday life; and how style is the only penetrating instrument of authentic 'realism', whatever the period.

I went many times to sit in the gallery of the Old Vic. There were four hundred excellent seats which at that time were sold for sixpence each. Every night they were filled with English working people. I went there once with some French friends. *Hamlet* was being performed in its entirety; it lasted four hours; the seats were wooden benches; it was a bit hard. But the audience sat there motionless. They were listening to the story of a national hero told by a national poet: that is always impressive. At the end my French friend asked me, 'Do you think they understand?' 'What?' I replied. 'The meaning of the play, the philosophy.' 'Oh,' I went on, 'certainly not. They have listened to the story which has unfolded in front of them as if it were a chronicle, a royal chronicle, in keeping with their traditions. They are fascinated by poetry, by sound, by rhythm' (which, by the way, my friends could appreciate even less than I). 'And that,' my French friends asked with a smile, 'is enough for them?' 'Probably they gather some kind of meaning,' I replied, 'their own individual meaning, and at the same time they enjoy being soaked in the words. It's a mysterious exchange, a sort of "osmosis", an intermingling of various elements in which sense cannot be separated from form. They are the voluntary victims of the power of incantation which belongs to poetry and which is no more and no less mysterious than the power of music.'

Here, you see, are two guides, two guards, two beacons – French classicism and English dramatic poetry – which have continually accompanied me on my journey through the contradictions of the modern theatre.

This journey is not an easy one, no more easy for the English or the French than it is, I imagine, for you Americans.

We live in the theatre as well as in life in the most indefinite, indeterminate period. And possibly the French and English suffer from this uncertainty more than you do because in the past we have been definite; in the past we have been determinate.

Now we feel uprooted. Believers or unbelievers, we cling to what convictions we have and we work; but our minds are in chaos. We don't know where we are going. Those who have kept faith and balance, observe this chaos; but it is not in their power to stop or organise it. Our best minds are given to analysing this period of disintegration.

At the present time the world presents us with a spectacle which is so passionately interesting and so full of anxiety that one wonders how the theatre can keep pace with it. You won't be surprised if I tell you that in this vast waste of anxiety France is as deeply involved as any. She has been materially, morally, and spiritually struck down. In fact she has never fully recovered from the 1914-18 war and the humiliation of defeat in 1940 has accentuated all her previous dissensions. We try continually to show the world that we are better than this defeat has shown us to be. It's a dangerous state of mind. And, to the sorrow of our best friends, I am sure it will be many years before we shall recover.

During the winter of 1957-8 in connection with certain events in North Africa, journalists and politicians in other countries spoke of French stupidity. That is something new; for we have generally been criticised for our excessive intelligence, what is called our incurable tendency towards intellectualism. Be assured, if you want to be, that intellectualism in France is not dead. We remain – and I say it with simplicity, for after all one must find one's strength where it lies – we remain intellectuals, and also artists. And the way in which we are reacting to our trials is particularly evident in our theatre.

For our theatre, like our society, goes in many different directions and it is only our traditions, which lie behind the contradictions, which tend to create any sort of unity. We are naturally exposed to the assaults of modern realism, including American realism: you know that your dramatists are played in France a great deal. We closed our doors to popular or bourgeois naturalism, a long time ago. Kitchens and bedrooms are banished from our stage. 'Parisian' comedy, so dear to our grandfathers, is all but dead. We have even been so determined to avoid presenting a photograph of real life on the stage that we made the mistake of ignoring Chekhov for many years. During the last forty years of course we have played Chekhov, but I believe that it is only in the last four or five years that the French public has felt Chekhov deeply, intimately. And now we welcome Chekhov but we have no use for his imitators.

Recently you have given a kindly reception in your theatres

to the work of two of our dramatists who have enjoyed long-standing reputations in France: Jean Giraudoux, who died to-wards the end of the war, and Jean Anouilh, who is younger and in perfect health. They are two very different writers who both began writing for the stage at the same time, in the thirties.

Giraudoux belongs to the tradition I have defined as classical. Fed upon the mythical sources of the Greeks he seems to be the heir to both Aristophanes and Racine. He has elegance and satirical wit. He is a writer with a style. For him, writing counts: he was unable to separate thinking from style: though some-times his style is a little precious.

Anouilh is a realist, often aggressively so, both in matter and in language. It is difficult to define Anouilh's style: while it moves from naturalism to expressionism, it is always darkly coloured by modern pessimism, the despairing sense of loss belonging to fallen angels. Anouilh's passion for absolute integrity, so difficult to achieve, has inclined him towards anarchy. This uncompro-mising attitude, which drives him to escape from a world of compromise, leaves in its wake a train of insults and invectives.

Here now is a pair of dramatists in striking contradiction. Paul Claudel died only a few years ago. He was a poet, one of the most powerful French poets we have known. Though anti-classical by position, he studied the Greeks and Shakespeare, he studied the Bible and the scriptures. He shaped a prosody and a syntax of his own. But because he is a Catholic poet his public tends to be specialised. Claudel always wanted in his work to remain outside actuality.

Now let us look at the other extreme: Jean-Paul Sartre, the existentialist, the promoter of 'littérature engagée' (committed), living in close touch with the events and values of our own time; and Albert Camus, a Nobel prize-winner, who was a disciple of

Sartre and then parted from him. The writing of Camus became increasingly classical, in the French sense of the term.

Now, to mention only the more important of the younger people, we have got Vauthier, a realist, who seems to be a kind of descendant of Strindberg, full of dreams and visions. We have G. Schehadé, the Lebanese poet, whose third play was produced by Jean-Louis Barrault in October, 1957. We have Jean Genêt and H. Pichette, both poets and realists. And finally there is the trio of the 'avant-garde', at present the most important group of all. Arthur Adamov, who in his most recent play *Paolo Paoli* seems to come near to Brecht; Samuel Beckett, who has been influenced by Joyce and Proust and who is related in his work to Kafka. His transcendental realism is close to the expression of modern anxiety in its most acute form, a sort of disease of the soul caught between the need for and the absence of God. Eugène Ionesco is the third representative of this 'Theatre in Hell', as one critic called it. Like Beckett, Ionesco uses a realism which makes use of invented characters, transplanted from humble areas of the world into a sort of Punch and Judy show where perfectly ordinary life disintegrates into nightmare. And very often this disintegration, which affects the language itself, makes us laugh. In Paris, while a rather small public is fascinated by Beckett, a larger one enjoys Ionesco as a comic dramatist, and laughs at his new world, the logic of which is curiously related to the feelings of a modern audience. The phenomenon Beckett-Ionesco is a very French one. Here we have two writers of foreign origin – one is Irish, the other Roumanian – both writing in French, and both born into the theatre in the intellectual Parisian atmosphere where their plays have not yet enjoyed great commercial success whatever their repercussions. And they are becoming known throughout the world.

Waiting for Godot was played for nearly a year on Piccadilly Circus, at the Criterion Theatre. I have just been to San Francisco: a group was rehearsing *Waiting for Godot*. I arrived in Los Angeles: I was taken to see a show – it was *Waiting for Godot*. You see the deep sort of realism practised by these two dramatists belongs to the world of poetry and of style. To penetrate to the heart of reality, far beyond appearances, they cannot make use of naturalistic methods.

In France those plays could not be born if behind the contradictions of our stage there was not some kind of basic unity between the intellectual movement and the development of the theatre.

Two men are leading the French theatre at present: Jean-Louis Barrault and Jean Vilar; they are both pupils of Charles Dullin, himself an actor in Copeau's company and one of his main disciples.

Here, in my view, is the main contribution of France to the theatre: men, and a tradition. We work within the framework of our classical tradition and under its constant pressure. We struggle to free ourselves: tradition has become not so much a guide as a constant provocation.

I have seen the same thing in England with the admirable tradition of Shakespeare, easier to adapt, I believe, to modern times.

For very many years in France tradition has quite logically been supported by institutions. Up to 1939 the state helped only the official theatres: Opéra, Opéra Comique, Comédie Française.

At the Comédie Française every generation can see the masterpieces of the past, French and foreign, together with revivals of the most important works of the last thirty years. From time to time there is a 'creation', because it would be fatal never to give a new play. The Comédie Française informs and provokes you: when you are young you are always against it; frequently it drags behind the times, so that at intervals it has to be brought up to date.

Up to 1935 all the unofficial theatres and companies were financed and supported by private money. The advent of the 'popular front' in 1936 brought more generous support from the state under the guise of popular education. But it must be said that while at the end of the nineteenth century there was a theatre building in France for every ten thousand inhabitants, most of them were transformed into cinemas between the two wars. Today, when Jean-Louis Barrault plays in Paris, he receives no grant from anybody. He is under the constant threat of bankruptcy.[1] What I find unique in France is that people of the theatre have always been ready to die for their art: and this is no pompous nonsense.

If today, in spite of invasions, in spite of wars, of political and economic disorders, there exists a living theatre in France, it is because in 1887 André Antoine, an employee of the Gas Company, opened the 'Théâtre Libre' with very little money: it was the beginning of naturalism ten years before Stanislavsky. Since 1913 men like Copeau, Dullin, Pitoëff, Jouvet, Baty, have taken upon themselves the *total responsibility*, financial and artistic, of their undertakings. This is no nationalistic outburst or uncon-

1. By André Malraux's famous decree of 10 April 1959, Jean-Louis Barrault was put in charge of Le Théâtre de France, the former Théâtre de l'Odéon, which since 1946 has been a part of the Comédie Française. By the same decree, Jean Vilar was put in charge of an experimental Theatre, both ventures to be subsidised by the State.

André Barsacq's s
Noé (**André** Obey),

André Barsacq's se
Viol de Lucrèce
Obey), Act IV

René Moulaert's
La Mauvaise Condu
Variot)

Michel Saint-Denis as
George Devine in
Famille (Jules Supervie

A scene from *Judith*

trollable French flourish: Pitoëff died before he was fifty, Jouvet and Dullin at sixty-four. None of the three retired. They were stopped by their heart or their kidneys while they were still acting.

Copeau and Dullin had schools attached to their theatres, not the kind of schools that exist to find jobs for pretty girls, or to bring money to star actors in decline. Not at all. Schools that cost money.

Barrault today is in the same heroic situation. But the state has partially taken the place of private capital. It gives to Vilar a theatre and a grant of 125,000 dollars a year. Moreover as the theatre has disappeared from the provinces since the coming of the cinema, the state has created five dramatic centres in the main areas of France. These centres play modern and classical repertory. They have a relationship with the universities, which in France do not have theatres. They are also in touch with the amateur movement. Each of them plays, at popular prices, three to six different shows a year, in anything between forty to eighty different towns, giving single performances in the smaller, and more in the larger. Repertory and presentation are generally of high quality. The T.N.P. (Théâtre National Populaire) plays at the price of little more than a dollar a seat.

These centres, together with the better touring companies from Paris, maintain the theatre in provincial France. It has been found that only by living and working in the heart of the provinces can artists and technicians generate a creative impulse. That's why the state does not subsidise touring companies. Instead, for instance, it sends people like me to Strasbourg to build up an organisation, with the help and participation of the local people themselves. Rooted in the provinces there is a chance that the organisation will slowly grow, calling upon and training local talent. In ten to twenty years' time we may find that this artistic initiative has helped to give expression to original talent in many parts of France other than Paris. Then the real goal of the theatrical decentralisation will have been reached.

The dramatic centres, together with men like Barrault and Vilar, are all far more concerned, I assure you, with modern plays than with the classics. Don't consider us a lot of old bores, obsessed with the past. That isn't true. But we are all trained in classical disciplines, having found that our modern theatre, with all its contradictions, cannot present us with a solid enough basis for development. A complete actor cannot take shape, a dramatist cannot grow out of photographic naturalism. True representation of reality requires transposition and style.

There is only one theatre. The Greeks, the Chinese and the Japanese, Molière and Shakespeare can provide food for our realism. True realists have made a great contribution to the interpretation of the classics.

I've finished. France has been my subject. I'm not doing propaganda for my country. I do not like nationalism in any form. But I want to seize this opportunity of thanking from the bottom of my heart those few people who having seen my work in Europe were instrumental in bringing me here. It has allowed me to discover a great country very different from what I had been told it was. It's a new stage in my later development, for which I am most grateful.

PART TWO

CLASSICAL THEATRE AND

MODERN REALISM

STYLE AND REALITY

TODAY, I would like to talk to you about 'reality in the theatre'. I have not chosen this subject by chance. I believe it has been imposed on me by the period in which we live, which has deeply shaken the very notion of reality. The comfort of deeply established reality, where conscience had its place, where God was in his heaven and in his church, where social classes were distinct, where moral law distinguished between good and evil – the whole organisation of an orderly world with its gradual changes has been upset by wars, by revolutions, and by discoveries of all kinds. It's a commonplace, in particular for us Europeans.

But you who are leaders in material and scientific progress are perhaps even more acutely aware than we what modern anxiety is: we are threatened in our existence, in our conscience, in our very integrity as human beings. We are witnesses of phenomena which very often we can no longer understand. We pinch ourselves to be sure we are not dreaming. There is a modern drunkenness, a modern world of wonders which dims our sense of values. To retain one's reality as a human being in such a world requires a sort of courage.

An artist lives within two kinds of realities. There is his humble human reality in which he shelters, and there is his reality as an artist, as a craftsman, which exposes him for much of the time, especially if he works in the theatre, to the public eye. There is unceasing conflict between these two realities. But one cannot become, or remain, an artist, if one is not first and foremost a man.

You do not know me. I do not believe that I am more of an exhibitionist than the average person in my profession. So before saying anything to you about reality in art, I would like to say a word about my own reality, my human reality, as frankly and discreetly as I can.

I am sixty. I have known the world as it was between 1900 and 1913 and I can remember it very well.

In 1914 I was seventeen, and one day, in 1916, I found myself in the front line in France. I finished the war in Bessarabia fighting against the Reds. At that time I saw Eastern Europe and most of the Middle East.

At the age of twenty-two I was the witness of terrible disorder, misery, and disease.

In between the two wars I got married, more than once. I had three children and the eldest fell at twenty, in Alsace, just below the mountain on the top of which I had been myself as a soldier of twenty.

The world changed for me once again in 1940. I was living in London. I was called up again and I went back to the army against my will. I had to go through Dunkirk to find myself again in London, where, by attachment and personal decision, I stayed. I directed the French team of the B.B.C.; in all, seven years outside the theatre and mixed up in politics.

Since then my daughter has made me a grandfather: to my dismay I find that I like it.

I lived and worked in France for the whole of my youth. At thirty-seven I went to England where I stayed for eighteen years, until 1952. Since then I have been living and working in Strasbourg.

I have travelled widely in Europe. Last June I was invited to go and see the Russian theatre: this gave me a chance to look at the Russians. I have been three times to Canada, but this is the first time that I have visited the States. The theatre once again has called me, but first I want to get to know the Americans, and at the end of this month I shall visit as much of the country as I can. I have been here for a week. I can't sleep much. I am aware of a sort of liveliness within me which makes me feel younger. To say any more about my human reality might be indiscreet.

Now may I say something of my theatre reality?

In 1919 I joined the company of the Théâtre du Vieux Colombier in Paris. Jacques Copeau had just come back from two seasons at the Garrick Theatre in New York. (He had opened the Vieux Colombier in 1913 when he was thirty-three but had had to close it in 1914 owing to the war.) So I was in a position to watch from its beginnings the movement that was to transform the French stage and have upon the European theatre an influence that is not over today; a movement that has proved to be more important than one could have believed even at the time of Copeau's death in 1949. Why was this? What gave such an impulse to this artistic revolution?

To begin with, it was a fight against naturalism as it had been started in our country by André Antoine. It was also a fight against the survival of romantic rhetoric in the interpretation of the classics, particularly at the Comédie Française. But it had an even broader and deeper purpose which was expressed by Copeau in his manifesto *Un Essai de rénovation dramatique* written in 1913. Reacting against many aspects of the theatre of that time, Copeau wanted to free the stage from cumbersome machinery and showy effects; to concentrate his efforts on the development of a new school of acting; and to give first place and importance to 'poets', by which he meant real dramatists, whether of the past or contemporary. It was in this spirit that he wrote at the end of his famous manifesto: *Pour l'oeuvre nouvelle qu'on nous laisse un tréteau nu* (For the work of the future let us have a bare platform).

When at the Vieux Colombier in the spring of 1920 Copeau gave a realistic play written by a 'poet', *Le Paquebot Tenacity* by Charles Vildrac, Antoine, the father of French naturalism, who had become a dramatic critic, wrote that he was astonished by the kind of 'reality' he saw on the stage. The floor of the stage was made of concrete. There was a proscenium but no footlights, and so no 'fourth wall'. *Le Paquebot Tenacity* takes place in a seaman's 'dive' in a small harbour. There was a door at the back through which the sea was suggested by means of light; there was a counter, three tables and ten chairs. That was all. And Antoine wrote, 'The atmosphere is created with an almost unbearable intensity . . . The public is no longer seated in front of a picture, but in the same room, by the side of the characters. This extraordinary impression has never before been produced to this extent: such a complete elimination of all "theatrical elements" makes for detailed perfection in acting.'

A little later Copeau gave the most 'theatrical' production of *Les Fouberies de Scapin* by Molière, set on a bare platform, built of wood, which was isolated on the concrete stage and violently lit by a large triangle of lights hung above it in full view. The actors played on the platform and around it. Such a disposition called for movement and speed, acting of a really physical kind, but at the same time the actors, exposed on that bare platform, had to give true 'reality' to their characterisations. Jouvet, who was little more than thirty, created an old miser of the utmost veracity.

A new reality had been brought to the interpretation of the French classics, a reality that had style, animated by a human, 'realistic' truthfulness.

In the autumn of 1921 the school of the Vieux Colombier was opened. The training was most unusual. The students, familiar with the theatre of the Greeks, of the Chinese and Japanese, with the Commedia dell'Arte, used to work most of the time without texts. Very often they wore masks. In fact Copeau used his young pupils as gifted children with whom, away from the influence of the much too normal actors of his company, he wanted to rediscover the secrets of acting, to experiment on new or renewed forms of dramatic expression.

In 1922 Stanislavski came to Paris with the Moscow Art Theatre. They played at the Théâtre des Champs Elysées. There we all went, all the students together, very smart, a little ready to laugh in advance: we were going to see those realists, those naturalistic people, the contemporaries of old Antoine! We saw *The Cherry Orchard* that night and we stopped laughing very quickly. There is a moment in the first act of *The Cherry Orchard* when all the characters return from a trip to Paris, worn out by days and nights in the train. They enter the nursery; Madame Ranevsky pauses to admire and feel the old room, full of memories, and Anya, her young daughter of seventeen, who has been brought up in that nursery, jumps on to a sofa and, crouching on it, is caught up by a fit of that high-pitched laughter which is induced by a combination of tiredness and emotion. And on that piece of wordless acting the audience of two thousand five hundred people burst into applause. Later on in the third act, Olga Knipper Chekhova, the wife of Chekhov, playing Madame Ranevsky, takes a cup of tea from the old servant while she is engaged in talking to someone else. Her hand shakes, she's burnt by the tea, drops the cup which falls on the ground and breaks. Fresh burst of applause. Why? Because the reality of this action was so complete, so untheatrically managed as to be striking even from a distance. It was enough to create enthusiasm. I had the opportunity of asking Stanislavski how he had achieved such balanced and convincing reality. He replied, 'Oh it's very stupid. She couldn't get it. We rehearsed for seven months but she still couldn't get it; so one day I told the stage-manager to put boiling water in the cup. And he did.' I couldn't help saying – I was twenty-five at the time, (but that man was wonderful) – 'Yes, that was stupid.' He laughed, 'It was absolutely stupid. But you have to do everything, anything, even stupid things, to get what you need in the theatre.'

Earlier that evening we had taken Stanislavski to see *Sganarelle ou Le Cocu Imaginaire* at the Comédie Française. It was a traditional production but there was an extraordinary actor in it, Jean Dehelly, already old, who revealed to me what lightness, what virtuosity can be reached by a juvenile in a classical farce. His performance was exquisitely true in its youthful artificiality – like a butterfly. But Stanislavski did not seem to appreciate this kind of acting. When we went out he said, 'You see my friends, we had a very good example tonight in that old theatre of what not to do.' That was all.

This visit of Stanislavski and his company was of incalculable importance to me. For the first time our classical attitude towards the theatre, our efforts to bring a new reality to acting, a reality transposed from life, were confronted by a superior form of modern realism, the realism of Chekhov. Stanislavski was then at his best; all the great names were in the company; the Russian Revolution was only five years old.

In 1931, after ten years of work and close collaboration with Copeau, I started my own company, La Compagnie des Quinze, at the Vieux Colombier. We rebuilt the stage on the assumption that Copeau had not gone far enough and that his permanent and formal setting was still too open to compromise. The new stage looked like a large room in a palace with visible sources of light in the visible ceiling and walls. Permanent columns would not prevent us from representing the sea, the banks of a river, a battlefield, as well as Lucrèce's bedroom. On the contrary this architectural disposition would emphasise our contempt for ordinary theatrical illusion. In fact, at the time we would have liked to get out of the theatre altogether. I thought seriously of taking a big boxing-hall in Paris, la Salle Wagram, and of playing there on the bare platform in the middle of the audience.

We had worked ten years together. We had developed a lot of possibilities as a company: we were mimes, we were acrobats; some of us could play musical instruments and sing. We could invent characters and improvise. In fact we were a chorus with a few personalities sticking out rather than actors ready to act the usual repertory, classical or modern. We brought to the Parisian theatre a specialised repertory of plays, most of them written by one dramatist, André Obey. We were single-minded. Our plays were of an epic character long before the style became better known. They dealt with broad popular themes; their plots did not turn on the psychological development of the characters. As actors we were sincere and resourceful; on the stage we gave the impression of being free, fresh, and real. A critic in Paris wrote that we brought 'nature' back to the artificial theatre-world of that period. We took London by surprise and by storm: maybe our genuine qualities pleased the English even more than they had the French.

During that period, 1931-1935, I directed all the plays – there were about ten – given by the Compagnie des Quinze, and acted in most of them.

In 1935, following the success of my company in London and its slow disintegration, I was asked to establish myself there. I drew up the plan of a school. The kind of actor I wanted was not to be found ready-made. Training and experiment seemed to me more important than the quick gathering together of a company without either meaning or unity. With the effective support of Tyrone Guthrie, the close collaboration of George Devine, and soon the help and friendship of Laurence Olivier, John Gielgud, Glen Byam Shaw, of Peggy Ashcroft, Edith Evans, Michael Redgrave, Alec Guinness, and of 'Motley', I opened my first school, the London Theatre Studio, a private school.

And now, on top of my French education I had to begin a new apprenticeship – in the English theatre, in the English themselves (not easy), in Shakespeare (more difficult still). After two years, at the invitation of Tyrone Guthrie, I had the daring to direct *The Witch of Edmonton* at the Old Vic, and a year later, in the same theatre, Laurence Olivier himself in *Macbeth*.

Intimacy with Shakespeare, living in Shakespeare's atmosphere, gradually introduced me to a scale of direction and interpretation infinitely broader than the one I had known in dealing with the French classical repertory. As the years went by I became familiar with Shakespeare's methods of composition, shaped to the architecture of the Elizabethan stage, and with a style of acting in harmony with the lyricism of Shakespeare's great poetical moments as well as with the realism of his popular comedy and farce. I had to follow all the variations of a language of which I tried slowly, painfully, to learn the scansion and to appreciate the rhythm.

In 1938 I had my first experience of realism when I produced *The Three Sisters* by Chekhov with John Gielgud's company.

Immediately after the war, in 1945, I greatly enjoyed producing Sophocles's *Oedipus Rex* with Laurence Olivier who at that time was one of the directors of the Old Vic. It was thanks to him that George Devine, Glen Byam Shaw, and myself succeeded in establishing the Old Vic Theatre Centre and the Old Vic School from 1946-1952, an enterprise of which I shall have more to say in a subsequent lecture.

Finally in 1953 I went back to France. I found again the French classical tradition as it was practised not only by the old masters, Charles Dullin and Louis Jouvet, but by the two newcomers, Jean-Louis Barrault and Jean Vilar, both of whom had followed the classes of Dullin, a disciple of Copeau. I also came into contact with the existentialism of Jean-Paul Sartre, the new atheist humanism of Albert Camus, and the transcendental realism of Ionesco and Beckett. In Paris I watched the success and growing influence of Bertolt Brecht, due I believe, rather to Brecht's qualities as a poet and craftsman than to his support by the Communist Party.

I have had the good fortune in our poor and devastated Europe to have had a great deal to do with theatrical architecture. In 1931, I rebuilt the stage of the Vieux Colombier with André Barsacq. In London I built and equipped two schools (1935 and 1947). In 1950 I contributed to the reconstruction of the Old Vic with the French architect, Pierre Sonrel. With the same architect

I built in Strasbourg, between 1953 and 1957, a modern theatre of eight hundred seats as part of an ensemble, where, for the first time in my life, I was able to assemble all the elements of a complete organisation – a small practice theatre, rehearsal rooms, workshops, and stores.

Such is my theatre reality, very quickly and superficially reported, almost reduced to the bare facts. I have been concerned with architecture, with the production of both realistic and classical plays, and with training – three aspects of the theatre closely related to each other.

And that brings me to the present.

You can see from the length of my story how my life has always been eaten up with work. It's a fact which I try to oppose more and more as I grow older. The theatre can be practised only with passion; but passion without detachment makes you blind and limits your life. Unless you are strong enough to conduct everything simultaneously – and I am not strong enough.

I have founded and directed three schools, probably because of a need to escape enslavement and find lucidity once again.

Am I above all a teacher? Some of my students tell me that I am sometimes cruel in my teaching. This would put me in fear of something within myself if I did not know what they mean. It's a certain way I have of working persistently to get what I have in mind; an obstinacy that takes hold of me when my health is good; the passion – that word again – of seeing something happen on the stage, and of creating the conditions which will allow this 'something' to happen naturally and continuously and not only by chance and in glimpses. But what is it that should 'happen'? What is it I am so eager to see 'happen'? Have I ever seen this thing 'happen'? Yes, from time to time, and when it does I never forget. That is why I still pursue it. I will try to explain what I mean, although in fact the whole of these four lectures are devoted to this explanation. It is my subject and in rather forbidding words it could be expressed in this way: a study of the conditions in which the interpretation of works of different theatrical styles can possess on the stage the greatest degree of reality.

Every country has its own reality, characteristic of its successive historical periods.

This national reality derives from the nature of the country and its traditions. Sometimes, however, this reality can be of a similar kind in a number of different countries at the same time. That is roughly what is taking place at the present time: with obvious differences between the various countries, realism, generally speaking, is the contemporary style most common to the whole world, and seems to be particularly thriving in its American and Russian forms.

At other times, movements in art, and particularly movements in theatrical art, appear to us like isolated monuments – the Greek theatre, for instance, the Spanish theatre of the Golden Age, the Elizabethan theatre, the Commedia dell' Arte, the classical French theatre of the seventeenth century. The classical theatre of the eighteenth century begins to show features common to all European countries.

I exclude from this picture the theatre of the Far East which has had, and continues to have, increasing influence on us.

The countries of Europe have found a certain individuality as a result of their accumulated traditions, of a super-imposition of periods which form a continuous chain of development; and at the same time they have influenced each other through their similarities as well as their differences.

For a Frenchman or an Englishman, there is a central tradition. It may be said that for the Englishman it is a popular and romantic tradition and that for the Frenchman it is an aristocratic and classical one. But not very far off we can see other traditions at work; the Italian tradition which springs mainly from the Renaissance; the great Spanish tradition which is nearly contemporary, in its origins, with the English; the German which was to develop later.

Another country enters the scene in the nineteenth century – Russia; and finally there is the American civilisation which blossoms particularly in the twentieth century.

The reality of each country is made of its historical personality which is constantly being modified.

The theatre takes part in the expression of that reality which is traditional in the case of old countries or fresh and unconventional in the case of new countries.

But the theatre is an art; and its form depends upon architecture, particularly on the relationship between the auditorium and the stage, on acting, and more than anything else, on the work of the writers.

The theatre's means of expression are forged by the time in which a play is written and performed, and by the contribution of the past.

In each country the theatre addresses itself to the public of its time which in due course will become a 'period'.

Each period has its own style even though we are not conscious of it as we live. (You know the impression we have today when we look at pictures of 1900, 1910, or even 1925. I can remember

Noah (**A**ndré Obey) at The
New Theatre, 1935, with Mar-
jorie Fielding, John Gielgud,
Marius Goring, Harold Young
and Colin Keith-Johnston

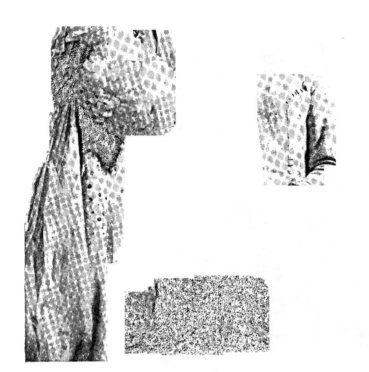

A scene from *The*
at The Queen's T
with Peggy Ashc
Redgrave, Harr
George Devine,
Shaw, Frederick
Guinness and Car

1925 very well and I never thought it would become 'a period'.)
And this style influences everybody. It has an influence on life
and it is with that unconscious feeling of the style of our own
time in our own country that we turn towards the interpretation
of the styles of different periods in different countries.

It is impossible to separate oneself from one's period without
danger of death. And it is impossible not to be influenced and
supported by the traditions of one's own country.

When an artist gives an interpretation of the works of another
period and another country, his interpretation is bound to
belong to his own country and his own time. He can try to understand what is past and foreign but it is utterly impossible to
capture the spirit of three centuries ago in a foreign land. One
day someone rang up Louis Jouvet and criticised his production
of a Molière play, saying, 'Molière would not have liked
that.' Jouvet answered, 'Have you got his phone number?' So a
contemporary artist will give his interpretation of the past from
the standpoint of today, on the basis either of traditions which
are native to him, or of a knowledge, a feeling, an appreciation,
which he has acquired for the reality of past periods and other
lands.

On the other hand, what is peculiar to our own time is the
speed and violence of the change which has affected every country in the world and tended to unify them. I say it again – in the
world of the theatre the common contemporary feature is
modern realism.

What is the nature of this realism?

We suffer greatly from doubt and instability. At the same
time modern discoveries have given us scientific means of in-
vestigation which have created in us an acute need for lucidity
and knowledge, a passionate desire to be no longer duped. This

D

astringent attitude forms the essential background of contemporary realism which assumes all kinds of aspects and applies to all sorts of subjects.

Between modern realism and traditional classicism, each with their national colouring, there is a clash; there are also strong reciprocal influences; there may even be the possibility of agreement: that is the important point.

The interpretation of works of the past is often approached with the same kind of anxiety, the same kind of lucidity, the same kind of astringency, which we bring to our comments on the present. In applying this scientific exactness to the examination of reality, and expressing our doubts about the very essence of this reality, we have been led to make an increasingly clear distinction between two kinds of realism. On the one hand we have the deep realism, which studies and expresses the nature of things, the meaning of human life, what happens behind and below appearances; and on the other, we have the realism that is satisfed with the representation of the external, the superficial realism which was called at the beginning of the present century 'naturalism'. If you will allow me, I would like to make a distinction between 'realism', which applies to the art of all times, and 'naturalism' which is an ephemeral form of art, belonging to the period of Zola, Ibsen, Strindberg, Antoine, Stanislavski, etc.

From a modern realistic point of view, certain periods in the past are closer to us than others. For instance, the English popular tradition as exemplified by Shakespeare is closer, I believe, to a man today, even to a Frenchman, than French aristocratic art of the seventeenth century as exemplified by the plays of Racine. If the Elizabethan dramatists have become fashionable in France since 1920, is it not because there is some kind of a relationship between modern and Elizabethan 'madness'? Is not surrealism evidence of this parentage?

But, in revealing a reality to which we feel related, those ancient periods used means of expression which are at variance with our contemporary custom. This has led us to wonder whether poetry in the theatre, a certain kind of poetry, is not a better instrument with which to penetrate reality than the broken prose of daily speech that is used in most plays.

We have now realised that style, by taking us away from the external forms of reality, from appearances, has itself become a reality, representative of a deeper world. In art the reality of a style has to be appreciated: it cannot be ignored or destroyed. There is a reality of ancient styles which is a part of human reality: a book and a play are as real as a cathedral or a statue, and, even if they are less concrete, they are nonetheless substantial. To have its meaning revealed a classical play must be acted in the reality of its style so far as we can understand and achieve it. You cannot interpret the past in terms of the language and style of today. From your modern standpoint you must assimilate the reality of past styles. There are not two worlds; there is not a world of the modern and a world of the classic theatre. There is only one theatre as there is only one world. But there is a continuity which slowly changes and develops from ancient to modern style. The deeper modern realism becomes in its expression as well as in its subject matter, the more it is possible to say that a modern actor, if he is brought up in a classical tradition which he has properly understood, will be better equipped to bite on modern forms of theatre.

There is a two-way action. The proper realistic approach we have today can be of great benefit to the interpretation of classical works. At the same time, training and practice in the classics is essential to enrich and inspire realism which is otherwise in danger of becoming sensational, sentimental or merely empty.

And to finish, a word about Russia. I told you that I was there in June 1957. I was officially invited with five other French directors and actors to visit the Russian theatre and see it at work in Moscow and Leningrad. We saw fourteen shows in fifteen days. We were very interested in Russian ways of directing, producing and acting; but we were even more anxious to get in touch with the people, to appreciate the conditions in which they lived, to discover something of their 'human reality'.

I found people in general and theatre people in particular openly expressing their need for contacts with the outside world. They wanted to develop. We heard them say both in private and public, 'We are thirty years behind the times in the theatre.' And it is true. But why?

For far too long the Russians have been compelled in the name of 'socialist realism' to practise exclusively the artistic creed which became official in the thirties – the 'Stanislavski system'. A system in artistic matters is obviously dangerous. I think that Stanislavski would have been the first to hate the idea that his way of working and of training people should be called a system. The man was the opposite of an intellectual fanatic: he was tall, strong-looking and relaxed. An impression of warmth, goodness, and passion emanated from him. He was a great master of the theatre of his own time and never confined himself to the narrow limits of 'naturalism'. I believe he would be the first to ask us to reject the system, only taking from it what is good for our time and country, and discarding the rest.

Realism, as I have seen it in Russia, has become academic, comfortable and bourgeois. Admirable in fragments but much of it is congealed.

This time I saw *Three Sisters* done by the Moscow Art Theatre and also an adaptation of Gogol's *Dead Souls* by the same company on tour in Leningrad. *Three Sisters* was what the Russians call a 'new production', meaning that it had been produced in 1940 by Nemirovich-Danchenko: and the company included some wonderful actors, but the three actresses playing the sisters were respectively 48, 50, and 52 – which is worse than at the Comédie Française.[1] It was a production of a very high standard, but it was Chekhov simplified both in style and meaning. The simplification of the out-of-door set for the last act was welcome but lacked unity. The play had been speeded up in tempo. Chekhov's famous pauses had been cut or shortened and consequently the 'atmospheric' noises, so dear to Stanislavski, were much less noticeable. The poetical values had been damaged in favour of a more optimistic, more clearly constructive meaning. Nostalgic melancholy, even despair, had given way to positive declarations. Vershinin's lines about what is going to happen in 'two or three hundred years' had taken on a truly prophetic sense. It was forced. The Russians claimed that at one time before the war their audiences had become bored with Chekhov and that they had had to renew their interpretation. Gogol was much better done. It was given in the original Stanislavski production. There were a lot of scenes with quick changes so that the sets were only sketched and not realistically detailed. Those giant actors, endowed with deep voices, gave full play to robust, colourful characterisations. In my view, one typical blemish did harm to the production. One scene in the play takes

1 Since those days the Moscow Art Theatre has played *Three Sisters* in London and Paris. The production had the same essential characteristics I had noticed in Moscow but many improvements had been made. In particular the three sisters were played by much younger actresses.

place during a storm. It was the most admirable storm! The thunder was unforgettable. And on top of it was the rain. Through the window on the right I could watch the rain go through all its phases: we had fast rain, slow rain, and at the end, remarkably, dripping rain. You could not only hear but *see* the rain, so much so that it was quite impossible to hear or see the play, which is not written in a realistic style.

But why did Gogol seem to stand the test of time better than Chekhov?

In spite of all my love for Chekhov, I suggest the reason may be that Gogol has a style which is more objective, more 'written', more classical than Chekhov's. It must be difficult to imitate Gogol. But goodness knows, Chekhov is being imitated all the time. The amount of simplified second-rate Chekhov to be seen in London and New York is remarkable – usually leading to a dull mediocrity which is called 'life'.

But theatre is not life. Theatre comes from life, but theatre is theatre: life in the theatre needs theatrical transposition, in writing and style.

In my next talks I'll try to show how in terms of architecture, direction, design and training this might be achieved.

STYLE AND STYLISATION

MY LAST TALK was called 'Style and Reality'. I spoke about human reality and artistic reality. At the end I said, 'Theatre is not life, theatre is theatre.' And I might add that theatre is a revelation: a concrete, intellectual, emotional and sensual revelation of life by means of this art which is called the art of the stage.

I also said, 'To reveal life the theatre cannot use the means of life. It has got to use the means of theatre.'

The Chinese say, 'It is not doors that are interesting, but what happens behind them: so why have doors?'

I also said the other day, 'The theatre needs transposition.' It needs 'writing'. To reveal reality it needs 'style'. I will try to suggest to you how this can be done in terms of architecture, of acting and direction, of design, and of training. Today I will devote myself to clarifying what we mean by style and showing you why it must not be confused with stylisation – that awful word.

The meaning of 'realism' is muddled and outworn. Only if it can be considered the best instrument with which to reveal human reality does 'realism' rise again to its former dignity; and then at the same time 'naturalism' declines.

What are the requirements of this regenerated realism?

Let us begin with architecture.

First of all the theatre building must put audience and actors in such respective positions that the play can be seen and heard; that the staging, in all its aspects, can be conceived by directors and designers in conditions which allow a feeling of reality to be created.

Æsthetic considerations alone cannot give us the right conditions. Theatrical knowledge and experience are quite as important as æsthetic and technical considerations if we are to achieve a theatrical architecture of real value. These considerations should originate from a need to stir in the public and in theatre people alike a spirit by which not only modern plays, but works of the past as well, will be brought to life in contemporary terms.

I say 'in contemporary terms'.

I know from books that in America a lot of work has been done in this direction. I have looked at the designs of Norman Bel Geddes and Robert Edmund Jones. I have not yet seen the theatre buildings themselves. In most European countries the auditoria of the theatres are out of date. I exclude the most modern theatres in Germany, and in Russia. The relationship between stage and audience is still governed by the social differences which have dominated our former societies, that of the eighteenth century in particular. The public is distributed in a number of tiers, usually between two and four, sharply separated from each other. But in modern gatherings, cinemas and sports grounds for example, the public has acquired the habit and the liking for being assembled in groups with very much less gradation. In our old theatres in Europe many people are badly placed for seeing and hearing. They are very often too far from the stage; and encouraged by film and television, they feel the need to be able to see and hear far more vividly. They need to be closer. The main anxiety of an audience is not only to be comfortable but to be placed in such a way that they can be 'reached' from the stage; that they can be struck by the reality of the performance they are watching. Audiences of today, or the younger part of them, do not care for operatic grandeur or fairy-tale illusion. They cannot believe in such things any longer. People nowadays are too 'realistic', too rational. And it is the same with the actors: cut off from the audience, they long to reach the public without being obliged to force their means of expression. They need to be placed in a position in which they can feel a sense of reality towards their audience.

I said, 'To bring works of the past to life in contemporary terms.' It is obvious that 'to give life to the works of the past' cannot mean 'reconstruction'. Reconstruction of the past is dead. Neither can we imitate the past. It has to be re-created from a contemporary attitude.

But the reality of a play derives first of all from the country and period where and when it was written. In terms of art the performance of a play depends upon the original scenic disposition with which the play is naturally, umbilically, connected. The scenic disposition of former theatres had a far more definite reality than the stage of today holds for the modern spectator. Consider quickly the Greek stage with its orchestra; the Spanish courtyard; the platform of the Italian Commedia dell' Arte; the pit and platform of the Elizabethan theatre; even the formalism of the classical French stage; and then turn your mind's eye for a second to the Chinese theatre or the disposition of a Japanese theatre for the performance of a Nō play.

In each case:

There is a close relationship between the visible shape of the stage and the form of the written play.

The relationship between stage and auditorium means both communion and distinct separation at the same time.

The stage is built of real material: stone for the Greeks, wood and a surround of curtains for the Spanish and Italians, painted wood and decorated interior for the Elizabethans – stone, decorated wood, drapes and chandeliers for the French.

This reality in the shape of the theatre and the material of. which the stage is made fits with an open, free and frank convention. The actor presents an invented action on a stage which everybody knows to be a stage. Illusion, or what is better, reality, is created by the actor. In due course, after the introduction of operatic machinery in the seventeenth and particularly the eighteenth centuries, we came step by step towards the modern stage. And it was the operatic stage with its magical illusion which became the instrument of naturalism at the end of the nineteenth century.

Electricity will give new possibilities to this elaborate machinery, already transformed by the use of modern materials – but to what purpose? Where drama is concerned, mainly to reproduce with a new perfection the appearance of real life. The requirements of the naturalistic theatre fit with those of opera. Verisimilitude as well as magic needs distance. Both depend upon a physical separation between the public and the stage. Illusion, openly created by the actor, is to be killed and replaced by life itself, real life, 'slices of life'.

The modern stage is empty; it has no meaning of its own. If you look at it in the afternoon you will see a dark hole ready to receive an infinite variety of life-like sets which at night will form a distant picture, set in a frame and isolated by the footlights. This more or less faithful photography of real life has created a new illusion which has deceived the public for an incredibly long time: the illusion that illusion has disappeared.

Naturalism is persistent everywhere, though in some countries more than in others. One is still justified however in asking the question – does the naturalistic convention offer us the most striking way of revealing human reality?

In other words, is the stage which we have inherited from naturalism the best instrument of modern realism, or not? It seems to be clear that our modern stage, not too remote perhaps from the needs of French classicism, cannot answer the requirements of all the other styles of the past. Its architecture is too different from the original theatrical dispositions, to which the plays of the past are umbilically attached. With the picture-frame stage, all plays of the Greek, Shakespearian, or Spanish traditions are distorted and robbed of part of their true reality.

Thus, our modern theatre is faced with a problem.

Naturalism has over-spent itself. It has lasted too long. Moreover it is wonderfully well served by the film. Our period has no proper style of its own except perhaps this kind of modern realism which, to judge from its beginnings in different countries, aims at the interpretation of human reality in its very essence, beyond and below appearances.

Our modern theatres should be able to house at the same time whatever kind of realism our contemporary conventions may require, together with major works of the past in their different styles, and provide them all with the right kind of architectural disposition. Our new theatres, our new stages can only be places of a transitional kind, adaptable to different needs, and serving as a common denominator between contemporary and classical works.

Hitherto the general tendency has been to begin from the old Italian stage and to place in front of it a proscenium and a forestage of a more or less transformable kind.

This stage can be of excellent flexibility. It can offer a multiplicity of acting areas, differentiation between which can be very much helped by lighting. Either the forestage is brought forward to increase the actor's contact with the public, or it is withdrawn, according to the style of the play to be performed. Thus the relationship between stage and auditorium remains changeable in detail, and ready to adapt itself to a variety of styles. So that the 'picture-frame' would become the exception rather than the rule.

Let us now take the second point and consider *acting* in its relationship both to classical theatre and modern realism.

To recapitulate, by classical I mean the long tradition that began with Greek tragedy and developed to its fullest extent in the seventeenth and eighteenth centuries. By realism I mean all that is attached to the school which began with Ibsen and Strindberg. I do not want to imply that the two are completely separated. They need not be opposed: very often they coexist. I would hate to encourage the idea that there are two forms of theatre: one which is wonderful and easy, called realism, and the other which is even more wonderful but almost impossible to accomplish, called classical.

In either case is the actor, director, designer, to behave in the same way or differently? Can the Stanislavski approach, for instance, apply to classical acting or not? Is the good realistic actor, provided he takes the necessary trouble, equipped to become a good classical actor?

To answer these questions without making dangerously arbitrary pronouncements, we must try to throw some light on what we mean by style. It may be a roundabout way but it is not avoiding the issue.

One says that a servant has style when he is obviously well trained and shows distinction in his behaviour. One says that a dress has style when its cut and colour are elegant. One also speaks of a 'style costume'. Here the idea of period comes in. A writer, even a contemporary one, may be praised for his style, and this appreciation is not necessarily connected with the idea of period. It's the same with an actor. Going into this a little more deeply we find that a French writer – it was Buffon, I believe – wrote, 'Le style, c'est l'homme même', which can be translated, 'Style is the man himself', meaning that the most authentic part of a man's personality, all that is deepest in him, is revealed by the style of his work.

So what do we find? That good manners, proper training, elegance, a sense of period, and finally this revelation of the personality – all these things are inherent in style. No wonder it is difficult to define.

To many people style suggests period; but that is a secondary meaning. It is evident that an actor who takes part in a realistic play of today can show style in his acting. Even scenes of drunkenness in *The Lower Depths* can have style. 'It's not the cowl that makes the monk.' To wear a period costume or even a stylish one may not give the actor style: it may do the opposite. Style is not something superficial or merely external. While it is closely related to form it cannot be reduced to form. It implies an idea of quality rather than of elegance; or, should we say, it implies quality before it implies elegance; and elegance in any case is not the right word.

We know contemporary writers who have got style and others who have not got it, whether they write in prose or verse.

The other evening I saw *West Side Story* and I found that the dance side of the show had a real contemporary style (not to mention the staging, which was equally remarkable). But I found the text was lacking in style. It was very often flat, so that the interpretation of the speaking parts in the play was not on the level of the dances.

It is sometimes difficult to be aware of the style that is taking shape in our time as we lead our daily lives. Style is like wine: better as it grows older. It also becomes more evident with time. Hence the confusion between style and period. I would like to suggest that the works of the past survive only if they have style, which means quality.

If we accept this notion, then we can define style as the perceptible form that is taken by reality in revealing to us its true and inner character. There is something secret about style. This perceptible or outward form holds a secret which we have got to penetrate if we are to perceive the essential reality which lies beneath it.

Let us be more simple and direct.

If we say that the style of a play becomes more evident with time, then, having classical works in mind, we must not confuse what is visible to us with the inner content of the play, or once again we shall confuse style with period.

On the other hand, we are accustomed to realism, with or without style, whether it is superficial or deep-rooted.

Let us take, for instance, a Shakespeare play. Here we are confronted with a text written in verse or prose. Being written in a language that we do not speak today it does not seem natural to us. And in addition the psychology of the characters, their mood, the way in which they are dressed, the way in which they move, their occasional handling of swords or daggers, all these things make it necessary for a modern actor to try to understand a manner of behaviour very different from his own, morally, intellectually, and physically. What must he do to be in a position to discover in the lines, and in the text, the human reality without the feel of which he will be unable to work in a convincing manner?

Let us deal quickly with the simple and elementary things which everybody can understand:

Knowledge of the period, historical conditions and customs.

Wearing of historical costume – a knowledge of the movement and possibly the dance of the period.

Handling of weapons.

All this can be learned through lessons and books.

Much more important and difficult than anything else is the text – the attitude of an actor faced with a classical text. To help you to appreciate fully the difficulty I will quote two short passages from Shakespeare. The first is from the Balcony Scene in *Romeo and Juliet.* You will remember that Romeo enters through the garden at night and Juliet appears at her window. Romeo speaks:

But soft! what light through yonder window breaks?
It is the east, and Juliet is the sun!
Arise, fair sun, and kill the envious moon,
Who is already sick and pale with grief
That thou her maid art far more fair than she.
Be not her maid, since she is envious:
Her vestal livery is but sick and green,
And none but fools do wear it. Cast it off.
It is my lady! O, it is my love!
O, that she knew she were!

She speaks, yet she says nothing. What of that?
Her eye discourses: I will answer it.
I am too bold, 'tis not to me she speaks.
Two of the fairest stars in all the heaven,
Having some business, do intreat her eyes
To twinkle in their spheres till they return.
What if her eyes were there, they in her head?
The brightness of her cheek would shame those stars,
As daylight doth a lamp. Her eyes in heaven
Would through the airy region stream so bright
That birds would sing and think it were not night.
See, how she leans her cheek upon her hand!
O, that I were a glove upon that hand,
That I might touch that cheek!

JULIET

Ay me!

ROMEO

She speaks.
O, speak again, bright angel! for thou art
As glorious to this night, being o'er my head,
As is a winged messenger of heaven
Unto the white-upturned wond'ring eyes
Of mortals that fall back to gaze on him,
When he bestrides the lazy-pacing clouds
And sails upon the bosom of the air.

You see – the text has a definite form. I've chosen it on purpose because it is very far from us. The lines about Juliet's eyes and the stars are examples of the artificial metaphors of the period.

Now I've said that when we come to act plays of the past we

can only give an interpretation emanating from the time and country in which we live. Does that mean that to fight against the remoteness of his text the actor playing Romeo has to create his own idea of the reality of the situation and suppose that he has jumped over a wall in the neighbourhood of Central Park or Marble Arch? If he establishes in himself such detailed conditions of time and place emanating from his everyday experiences, is it not likely that he will become aware of a clash between the modern reality and the lyricism of the lines? Won't he feel much more 'natural' if he allows himself to make pauses by neglecting or exaggerating the punctuation of the text and the shape of the verse?

Now let me quote my second piece. It's from *Macbeth*, the last act.

MACBETH

What is that noise?

SEYTON

It is the cry of women, my good lord.

MACBETH

I have almost forgot the taste of fears:
The time has been, my senses would have cool'd
To hear a night-shriek: and my fell of hair
Would at a dismal treatise rouse and stir
As life were in't; I have supp'd full with horrors,
Direness, familiar to my slaughterous thoughts,
Cannot once start me.

Re-enter SEYTON

Wherefore was that cry?

SEYTON

The queen, my lord, is dead.

[65]

MACBETH

She should have died hereafter;
There would have been a time for such a word.
Tomorrow, and tomorrow, and tomorrow,
Creeps in this petty pace from day to day
To the last syllable of recorded time;
And all our yesterdays have lighted fools
The way to dusty death. Out, out, brief candle!
Life's but a walking shadow, a poor player
That struts and frets his hour upon the stage,
And then is heard no more. It is a tale
Told by an idiot, full of sound and fury,
Signifying nothing.

I've quoted those famous lines for one simple reason. When you come to a line like 'Tomorrow, and tomorrow, and tomorrow', your desire for truth will incline you to cut it into three definite parts so as to avoid a conventional delivery. But what is the result? The meaning of 'Tomorrow, and tomorrow, and tomorrow' carries a sense of eternity. With long pauses, the second 'and tomorrow' may sound like tomorrow morning and the third may be placed a month or so later. This absurd reality may be due to an excessive importance being given to the punctuation which breaks the unity of the line. It is a small matter, but, taken together with the example from *Romeo and Juliet*, it illustrates a point of great consequence.

Style has its own reality: it is made up of a choice of words, of shape, of rhythm and emphasis. This artistic reality cannot be separated from meaning. Besides, it often has a meaning of its own. It must not be broken or altered, but penetrated and deciphered if the human reality contained in the text is to be brought out fully.

A play written in verse, even in good prose, is like a score, but it is susceptible to a less exact reading than music, for it is not based on a similar kind of mathematical scheme. One should get used to reading the play at sight with a sharp eye, attentive to precise notations, alert and responsive to every indication of sound and rhythm.

Is that enough? Certainly not. Without dramatic motivation such a reading might only lead to a more or less beautiful declamation of the text devoid of much meaning. It would be unlikely to produce convincing acting. Psychological, social, emotional reality must be called upon to give substance to the form. At the same time the actor, who depends upon his own resources, must not accumulate all the elements of a contemporary reality *outside* the style and so create a conflict between reality and style. We have seen that if the form is destroyed or altered, the sense is also destroyed, and the right sort of revelation will not be produced. Perhaps another revelation might result, perhaps of an even more interesting kind, but it won't be the reality which the poet tried to express in his text. In a play of style, sense cannot be separated from form. A living respect for form, sensitivity to poetical colour and to rhythm, are essential to the kind of intensified drama which a classical actor, faced with a character, has got to create.

Faced with a character: we are coming to the crucial point. How, through a formal text, is an actor going to come to grips with his character?

Here I think one must be extremely cautious because this operation is the most difficult of all, yet at the same time so fascinating that it justifies all Stanislavski's efforts to explain and clarify the process. Tired of clichés, tired of routine, he analysed what happens inside a great actor. He drew from his own experience and from watching other actors. He studied actors at work and tried to elucidate the mystery of their behaviour as artists and craftsmen. He wanted to put order into an actor's approach to his rôle, to rationalise it—hence his 'system' or 'method'. During the time when 'an actor prepares', what part is played by observation, by external circumstances, by emotional memory? How can mechanisms and habits be created so as to liberate the subconscious? What help is to be expected from action, physical action?

All this in Stanislavski is perfectly good and illuminating, and and it is not surprising that American actors should have adopted Stanislavski so closely. He answers American needs. He came to your help at the beginning of your tradition, which is a realistic one.

Let us go further. Stanislavski, like Copeau in another direction, was a reformer. He was reacting against the theatre of his time. And in his time he saw the end of the romantic period and the beginning of naturalism. His contribution was to raise the level of naturalism to that of true realism.

But he did not always succeed. He was sometimes a victim of his 'period'. Do you know the published production of *Othello* by Stanislavski? Here the motivations are often naturalistic. The reality of Shakespeare's style does not seem to be taken into consideration.

In a classical play the actor must not hurry or jump upon the character. You must not enslave the text by premature conception or feeling of the character. You should not hurry to get on the stage and try to act, physically and emotionally, too soon. Psychological and emotional understanding of a character should come through familiarity with the text, not from outside it. You must know how to wait, how to refuse, so as to remain free. You must be like a glove, open and flexible, but flat, and remaining flat at the beginning. Then by degrees the text, the imagination, the associations roused by the text penetrate you and bring you to life. Ways are prepared for the character to creep in slowly and animate the glove, the glove which is you, with your blood, with your nerves, with your breathing system, your voice, with the light of your own lucid control switching on and off. The whole complex machinery is at work; it has been put into action by the text; now it can be usefully helped by Stanislavski – without his system – please.

The course to be followed by classical acting, if I see things rightly, is therefore different at the beginning from the course to be followed by realistic acting. But both in the end come down to the same laws which the demands of modern realism have strengthened. These demands are good. They make for sincerity, simplicity, for clarity of meaning.

Finally I must answer the question, 'Is a good realistic actor equipped to become a classical actor?'

There is no separation. Both require the same acting but a different approach.

Classical art requires, even in the smallest parts, the appropriate knowledge and practice of styles. One cannot act the classics without practice; practice in the relationship between a distant language and the too-familiar reality inside you.

Classical theatre also requires a strong and controlled sensibility.

Most of all it demands well-trained actors with good means of physical expression. The most important qualifications are the size and proportions of the body, and the size, quality, and range of the voice. Needless to say that all this should go together with a good artistic sense and temperament. In essence, there is no difference between classical and realistic acting. It's only that they do not take place on the same level, which is probably why classical art imposes the need for greater severity in the selection of actors.

Classical plays present us with many passages which are dead or empty. Beauty of form has prevailed over matter. If those passages are not cut, then virtuosity is required of the actor and the special ability to make what is formal and shallow appear credible and attractive.

We have seen that the handling of style presents us today with many problems. I wonder whether it is embarrassment that has brought about stylisation? It's an awful word, but what else is there? I have heard theatre people ask each other, 'should the production of this play be realistic or would it be better "stylised"?' In this sense, stylisation seems to be opposed to photographic realism. Sometimes this is so – a lamp-post to symbolise a street in the slums, and generally speaking, a selection of elements which can be representative of con-centrated reality. Expressionism has a lot to do with it.

What is dangerous about stylisation is its vagueness. It is connected with experiments in a large variety of directions. It can affect the look of things and even become synonymous with decorative fashions. The invasion of the stage by cubism and the plastic arts has resulted in stylisation. It goes hand-in-glove with fantasy and 'having fun'. If you are afraid of the seriousness of a play you 'stylise' it. There is a jocular aspect to stylisation, a tongue-in-the-cheek attitude. How many Restoration comedies of true style do not, when stylised, become caricatures or parodies?

I prefer style, the authentic style, treated freely, without self-consciousness. Style is not frightening: it is enjoyable. Through style we can approach the past in its richest vein. Style lasts. Style does not lie. It is the expression of real understanding, of deep communication with the world and its secrets, of the constant effort of men to surpass themselves.

One must love style. Style is liberation from the mud of naturalism.

STYLE IN ACTING

DIRECTING AND DESIGNING

THE WORK OF THE DIRECTOR in the theatre is sometimes exaggerated, sometimes disparaged, but it is on the director's work that the theatre producer or manager still depends to make as sure as possible that a play is going to be a success. He also depends of course on the star-actor; but he does not depend on the actor at the expense of the director. A theatrical production needs the director's talent, his personality, his imagination, his power of attraction, his authority over the actors and all the other people who collaborate in the show. It needs the confidence which he can inspire. The director is the centre of the organisation, he is the link connecting together all the elements which are involved in a modern production and which being more specialised than ever before, have a tendency to fall apart. He stands for unity, he is the guarantee of intelligence, of efficiency, of quality. I am a director myself!

During the last fifty years theatrical conditions have raised the director to an intoxicating position. Hated, flattered, beloved in turns, he has enjoyed so many privileges that one is hesitant to speak about them.

It has been said that during the first half of the present century directors have made a more creative contribution to the theatre than the dramatists.

In dramatic literature the period was not a very productive one, and it is clear that when plays are made of the sort of literature which is antipathetic to the stage, and when dramatists are more attracted by ideas than by people, then the director, living and working as he does amidst scenic realities, has the game in his hands.

Although it may be a debatable point, it would seem that the innovations and changes which have transformed the theatre since the end of the nineteenth century have been due primarily to Antoine, Stanislavski, Gordon Craig, Adolphe Appia, Granville Barker, Max Reinhardt, and Jacques Copeau, rather than to Ibsen, Strindberg, Chekhov, Shaw, Pirandello, Claudel, Giraudoux, or O'Neill. Those directors were 'reformers': they dealt with every aspect of the theatre: they did much to change the form of the theatre in which they worked.

During the last fifty years we had seen the contribution of the Music-hall, the experiments of the Russians in the twenties, the discoveries of Jean-Louis Barrault in adapting the works of Faulkner, Knut Hamsun and Cervantes, and the imaginative ideas of W. B. Yeats who was both a poet and dramatist; today we see the development of musical comedy, the success of Marcel Marceau, and the work of Bertolt Brecht who was also a scenic reformer, though he is still too close to us for the real nature of his contribution to be clear; and above all we have the achievements of the cinema where the director has almost replaced the author: all this, in one way or another, underlines the importance of the field in which directors have shown their influence. It all belongs now to theatre history and has been recorded in books; but what has not yet been said, and what I believe to be true, is that this period of the director's supremacy is beginning to pass, anyway in Central and Western Europe.

The tendency in Europe, and very particularly in France, is now to deny that the director is what is called a creative artist.

I can see the same tendency in London. The policy of an active theatrical organisation in London, the Royal Court Theatre, which shelters the English Stage Company, is resolutely to give first place to the dramatist. The Company is organised to stimulate the writing of as many contemporary plays as possible. Simple methods of staging these plays, far from spoiling them, should enhance their qualities. Meetings with young dramatists take place on Saturday afternoons. Ideas and criticisms are exchanged. Numerous people are constantly at work reading plays. I suppose you felt the same need when you established the Playwright's Company in America?

What is the reason for this tendency? Is it simply a swing of the pendulum? I have already emphasised – for it is one of the themes of these lectures – that our period has a realistic character. Obviously the theatre as a form of entertainment will go on. It will always go on. But even the connotation of the word 'entertainment' has now changed considerably. People are becoming increasingly concerned with what a play means. When I look at the theatre list in the American papers I am struck by the development of the off-Broadway shows. And on Broadway itself... I don't say the meaning of the plays is always satisfactory, but I do say that the meaning is there, and it is on the meaning that the emphasis is put, even in musical plays. *West Side Story* is not simply entertainment. The dance part, which is the most interesting, has a meaning. Since the war, there has grown up a kind of necessity for contemporary works which deal with the position of man in modern society. This trend is equally evident in the English and French theatres.

And this need for a meaning, whether human, moral, social, or even metaphysical, is naturally connected with a liking for realism, for reality in all its aspects. And this liking for reality goes right against sheer exhibitionism, and entertainment for entertainment's sake. It goes against the spectacular director. It demands plays which have something to say.

But to say something effectively in the theatre one needs two things: substance, and the means to express it. In our transitional theatre the dramatists are like the architects, the scene designers and the directors: they are all in search of forms, of methods of transposition, of style.

If then plays are to come first, let us look at their evolution before we examine the work of the director any further.

To express modern reality in all its complexity we have to discover new forms: hence, our curiosity, our intensive study of the past, our new theories and manifestos. Painters and sculptors have done it before us – the theatre always comes last – but now, finally, we are open to all sorts of influences.

First and foremost, the influence of the Far East; of the Chinese and Japanese theatres which, for poetical purposes, invented the revolving stage and the wonderful bridges projecting into the auditorium; instruments to relate space to the passing of time, not used at all for the purposes of practical realism.

In Japan we find the Nō players and the Nō play, its stage surrounded by the public on three sides, its costumes which are built on the actors like a piece of architecture; with its choruses of singers and musicians, with its feeling of eternity.

The modern theatre, following Bertolt Brecht, likes to be called 'epic' and the word has met with considerable success in Europe. But that is only one aspect of a world-wide movement which was started under the influence of the far-eastern theatre. Yeats was first in the field. Thornton Wilder anticipated Brecht when he wrote a play like *Our Town*. And most of André Obey's plays, written for the Compagnie de Quinze, like *Bataille de la*

Marne and *Loire*, can be called 'epic'.

And now we must look at our own classics from the same point of view.

We do not go back to our classics simply out of respect for the past. We do not want to be congealed by our respect. By looking at the Greeks, the Spaniards, the Elizabethans, by looking at Shakespeare as well as at the Chinese and Japanese theatres, we are trying to find resources for our modern world, for our modern art, our modern theatre. We are trying to rediscover secrets of composition, of construction, of language, we are trying to rediscover what is meant by form in order that we may express substance: for modern realism needs new instruments with which to reach the heart of reality. We want to develop realism, not to kill it. There is only one theatre and it is in constant evolution as times goes by.

There is no question of acting all the classics. To put on the whole of Shakespeare from first to last, systematically, seems to me the most discouraging undertaking. In suggesting that we make a choice, let us select those classics which can be of concern to us today.

This return to the great works of the past must be achieved in a way that will attract not only scholars but a good proportion of the general public. It requires knowledge and appreciation. It should be part of a policy. It demands conviction and skill from manager and director alike.

Let us now consider the director and direction.

The first problem for a director is to select a play. The choice is important and should have an idea behind it. I have often seen the following extraordinary situation. A director is rung up and asked to direct a play. He reads it, he doesn't like it, or not much, and he says yes, finding in his indifference a sort of professional virtue because it's good to do what you don't like (as if the absence of love could lead to an increase in lucidity). But without initial impulse the production may be tepid and lack conviction. It seems to me that the success of a production depends first of all on the shock the play gives you when you read it through. Nothing can replace this initial impact, this first revelation. It may be confused or mysterious, but you will always have to come back to it for guidance. It works on you both as an incitement and as a brake. The difficulty is not to have ideas – the imagination of the director is generally fertile – but to check one's ideas. If you jump on your ideas, like the actor who takes hold of his character too quickly, you are in danger; you may see only one side of the play; you may simplify or systematize.

Let the play come to you. Read it again and again, and not in a fragmentary way. Try to read the play for the first time at a single sitting so as to get the feeling of the whole. Then go on reading it till the play speaks to you, until you can remember easily the sequence of events, the main movements of the text and the connecting passages, until you know clearly where the play is weakest and strongest. Delay for as long as you can thinking about the production itself.

I won't try to make a definition of production. It can't be done. It has been attempted many times. There are as many ways of directing as there are directors. It's an empiric and a personal matter.

My purpose is to consider the production of a big classical play in a style that is remote from us, a Shakespearian or a Greek play, for instance. Here the problems of production are the broadest, the most tangible, yet the most puzzling and fascinating at the same time.

When faced with a great work of style, the director is in a complex position. He must be submissive and creative at the same time. In other words if he is to succeed in being both faithful to the work and efficient in his treatment of it, the director has to substitute himself for the dead dramatist and re-create the play.

It is very difficult to find one's way into the right sort of submission and to remain alive, inventive and inspiring to others.

Submission should not lead to a ready-made, scholarly, or pedantic attitude.

On the other hand invention doesn't mean fantasy. To let one's imagination loose, to please oneself, to follow one's own inclinations, may not result in true invention but in an imposition, an exhibition of personal ideas and moods, however original or brilliant they may be. I believe that the time of the Hamlets in modern dress, of the Oedipus complex psychologically applied, of the sensational opposition of styles, is over. Let me give you an example. A production of *A Midsummer Night's Dream* is under discussion. 'Wouldn't it be fun to do *The Dream* in nineteenth-century costume,' says the director, 'with a chorus of flying fairies and Mendelssohn's beautiful music?' All such kinds of stylisation and fantastication are out of date. We need something deeper, closer to the dramatist's work than this flippant approach. What we want is a union between the meaning, the heart of the meaning, as it may be felt by modern man, and what I have called in a previous talk, the reality of the style which cannot be separated from the meaning.

Reality of style is composed of what elements?

Of construction and composition. Composition in musical terms. Construction considered in all its different parts and the way in which they are connected.

Of rhythm. Relationship between the different rhythms first taken in big chunks.

Of the tone and colour of the language, and how the text goes from one tone to another.

There is no meaning or psychological construction in a play which can be separated from its style. The one contains the other. Style has its own meaning. It is through, not apart from, text and style that meaning and psychology should be analysed. A Freudian or a mystical Hamlet would be in danger of being prosaic or exalted, because such an interpretation would come to the director's mind apart from the reality of the play's style. An imposed motivation or interpretation, simplified or systematic, will not harmonise in the actor with the varied requirements of the text or its power of incantation. The text has its own power, it creates its own effect: it must not come into conflict in any way with psychological motivation. This is the most thrilling problem that modern actors and directors have got to solve. On its solution depend the greatness and strength of impact of the production.

It is from the director's solitary study of the text, reading and re-reading it, discovering meanings that are revealed by the play's composition, noting rhythm, colour, and tone, that he will slowly begin to realise how to cast the play: temperament of the actors, their complexion, stature, and most important for classical plays, the quality and strength of their voice, together with the essential contrasts between them – all this will gradually become clear. There is a relationship between the casting of big classical plays and the casting of operas. At the Comédie Française, following the traditions of the French classical theatre, the actors are still classified according to their types, temperament and vocal ability. The French word is 'emploi' and these 'emplois' include fathers, juveniles, soubrettes, first and second valets, and so on, a practice which may go against 'human reality' to an excessive extent but is naturally in line with 'artistic reality'.

During the initial phase of the work, the disposition of the play on the stage should also reveal itself to the director. First, the general lay-out: which scenes should be played where – at the back, front, side – it's a sort of geography that has to be completed early on, in the form of a plan showing the main moves of the characters, their entrances and exits: a traffic plan. This early process of adapting to the stage the broad architecture of the play should not at first be restricted by detailed, psychological motivations. The play must breathe freely. Its flow must not be interrupted on the modern stage any more than it was on the Elizabethan stage, to which it remains umbilically attached, where 'architecture was like frozen music'.

The unfolding of the play, the 'geography' of the scenes, the 'traffic': from these three essentials, the lay-out of the set with its main changes should be evolved in collaboration with the designer. We are not designing scenery yet: we are planning how to use our space. We shall get on to the choice of shape and colour very shortly. But this choice should not be dictated by decorative so much as by dramatic, emotional, and practical considerations. Its success depends upon the balance maintained by designer and director in their vital collaboration. Complete freedom in the exchange of ideas is certainly fruitful provided that the director knows what he wants and is not gradually dominated by the

Oedipus Rex with Laurence Olivier. Old Vic Company at The New Theatre, 1945

Above, the re-built
designed by Pierre Sc

Left, Le Centre D
de l'Est Strasbourg.
the stage designed
Sonrel, 1957

designer's talent or usefulness. One does not go to a designer to get one's production smartly or appropriately furnished and dressed, nor to be presented with sensational scenery and costumes that will unbalance the production and obliterate the actors. It is a fact that many productions are indirectly directed by designers. As for scenery, its form and its colour should give a play both its background and a kind of spring-board to the action. Well-dressed actors will do the rest.

But the designing of costumes is going to face us with the most acute problems. First a general one. What do we expect from costumes? To what sort of use are they going to be put, particularly in a classical work?

I was very surprised on one occasion when I saw *As You Like It* with scenery and costumes in the style of Watteau. Why not? 'Wouldn't it be fun to do *As You Like It* in the style of the eighteenth century,' said the imaginary director I have already mentioned. But there was more to it than that. The legs of the leading actress were far from perfect. 'In Watteau style they will be hidden.'

I won't discuss the suitability of eighteenth-century style for *As You Like It*. It was fun of the most dusty sort. What seems to me dangerous in a case like this is to see a play's style subjected not only to a different period but to the individual manner of a well-known painter of that period. The style of a period, even of a painter, may be a necessary inspiration, but the moment you begin to bring on to the stage the copy of a masterpiece, you will produce great visual effect perhaps, but almost certainly dramatic lifelessness. You copy instead of inventing. You transform the theatre into a museum. How could a costume so copied have value for a particular play? The actor is in disguise: he is not dressed. Moreover the anachronism may be striking, but it is not original. It's fun and nothing more than fun. There may be a certain revelation in such a stunt, but how can it suit the secret style which lies at the heart of Shakespeare's play?

A costume is first of all made to be worn by an actor. It should help the actor to act physically, without trying to impose a character upon him. Otherwise the actor is imprisoned by his costume. A designer should know what it feels like to wear a costume and to have to act in it. A good costume makes you feel free and carries you further into the character at the same time. In addition to this, on any given set, it should establish good relationship, in shape and colour, with the background. Sets and costumes, lightly designed, should help the actors and the public to capture the overall character and emotional impact of the production.

There is also the question of lighting, but that is too complicated a subject to be dealt with now. In a classical production with quickly moving scenery, lighting is of first importance. It can help, often unaided, to suggest changes of location as well as mood.

The rest depends upon acting and the strength of your original conception. Discipline, essential when you are at work, is the condition of freedom in acting. Freedom of the director, freedom of the designer, freedom of the actor: it's impossible to achieve one without the other. Without this common freedom I believe that complete reality in acting cannot be achieved.

I am not assuming an easy attitude towards the idea of freedom. To attain freedom is a life's work. We mark with a white stone the few productions during the preparation of which we have had the feeling of being free and of making other people free. Four times in the course of my life I have had the experience of leading a company in such a way that the last dress-rehearsal took place without any tension, in a spirit of confidence which was justified by public success the next day. This kind of freedom means mastery.

What concerns me most, in the present state of the theatre, is how to attain this freedom and how to ensure that it is something usual and familiar.

The first condition necessary to create this freedom, without which dramatic reality cannot be complete, is to have a stage in keeping with the style of the play: picture-frame for naturalism and certain forms of realism, or even certain classical plays: all plays which need, more or less, the illusion of life being lived. But for the rest we need a stage of the kind I tried to describe in my last lecture, liberated, openly conventional, where the theatre is theatre, where the actor is an actor and the dramatic action an invention in which the public is made to believe.

There is no possible freedom, I believe, if the people working together on a show have not previously known each other. I come back to that human reality which is indispensable to artistic reality. To me the unity and quality of a performance, particularly if the play is one of style, depends mainly on a quality and a unity which should exist in the company before the work on the play begins. A director must know the elements of his realisation, and the means by which he is going to bring the play to life, before he sets to work on it. He must know his collaborators, particularly his actors, but also all the people, even the least significant, who will take part in the preparation of the show behind the scenes. (Think how important a stage-manager can be.) It's from that mutual knowledge and pre-existing understanding that strength can freely spring and an artistic conception be rooted in firm ground.

I will probably be accused once more of going against the

times. I have been accused of training people for a theatre that does not exist. I am aware of that criticism. I am told that the people who work in the theatres of the West End, the Parisian Boulevard, and Broadway are a great family, all of whom know each other – actors say so with tearful voices. And we find that up to a point it is true, especially as we come towards the end of our life.

But it is also perfectly false. The only style this great family can touch is the realistic one. Look, however, at Stanislavski; look at the American Group Theatre. Did they not bring something new to realism itself? Will not their names go down in theatrical history because they were based on an attempt at permanence and continuity?

What happens with plays of great style?

I do not know if you feel like we French. We often complain that, even in the same show, actors play in many different styles. How could it be otherwise when there is such a variety of styles; when actors have got to be able to move from Shakespeare to Clifford Odets and thence to television?

Unity of style can be obtained only by working together and getting used to each other's physical and emotional reactions. Occasionally one may succeed without it and directors and actors of genius delight in winning against the odds: it's so much more exciting! But a theatre cannot establish an artistic policy unless it gathers together a well composed group of collaborators around a permanent company of actors, with partial renewal every year. Even with a variety of interesting plays the talent of a director is not enough to give expression to a policy without the continuity of the actor's presence. For it is the company that gives the place its spirit. The public is attached to the men and women they can see in the flesh.

That was a digression. To conclude I return to my subject.

What is the working relationship between actors and their director going to be?

This is an embarrassing question. I am at the moment changing my mind towards it and I could not begin to answer it without taking you into my confidence.

I have always been caught between two opposite tendencies: on the one hand to give shape, to give plastic value to a production; on the other to preserve the freedom of the actor.

I believe that the layout of a set, the relative positions of the actors, their movements, attitudes, the expression of their bodies, the sound of their voices, have by themselves a power of direct revelation.

I have studied Greek and Far Eastern theatrical forms. I have a strong feeling for tragedy, enough to want my staging to have formal value. The use of space on the stage has a precise significance for me: two steps to the right, two steps to the left, such a small move can be full of meaning. From feeling strongly the need for such a move to imposing it upon the actors, is a very little distance; but to make an actor appreciate such a need, you must suggest it at just the right moment in just the right way, even with somebody who has absolute confidence in you.

Add to this, that as an actor, I have often practised improvisation, rehearsing and playing in the manner that the Italians call 'alla improvisare'. There is a medium in which the actor invents everything within a given framework. He is not directed, he is rather 'advised' from the front by a director who acts as a kind of mirror. This sort of freedom, as I experienced it on the stage, was the most liberating experience.

How is one to reconcile these two ways of working, to give expressive shape to a production, and at the same time to cultivate the actor's inventive freedom? There lies the secret of theatrical art. But I have not yet put my hand on its solution.

I have been spurred on in my search by a man who is nearly twenty years younger than I am, Jean Vilar, the head of the Théâtre National Populaire in Paris[1]. A few years ago he created the Avignon Festival, which is now an important yearly event. He is the man I most admire in the French theatre today. I have acclaimed his two productions of *Le Prince de Hombourg* by Kleist and *Don Juan* by Molière. He has a strong theatrical organisation, the best collaborators on every side, and a permanent company. His theatre, the Palais de Chaillot, is not a suitable one, but it has two thousand five hundred seats. Vilar has taken advantage of this abnormal size to play at popular prices and to reproduce indoors the open and free conditions he finds at Avignon. There is a very large stage which he has enlarged still more by building a forestage over the orchestra pit, thus connecting stage and auditorium. He plays without footlights. His open stage is lit by spots set in the auditorium, and he never lowers a front curtain between audience and actors. When I saw his work for the first time I was very surprised by the daring way in which he makes use of space, limiting it by means of lighting. Scenery for him is only a background. His costumes are generally designed by painters, not by stage designers; they build up the actor by means of strong blocks of colour without unnecessary details. He makes considerable use of music and sound. For ten years before his appointment to the T.N.P. he played Strindberg, Pirandello, Chekhov, and any number of modern plays. He was trained at Charles Dullin's school in classical disciplines, but by

1. Since these talks were given, Jean Vilar's company has been seen both in London and New York.

nature he is a Latin realist, born on the shores of the Mediter-
ranean. He interests and puzzles me because he has very often
succeeded in achieving that difficult fusion between a realistic
attitude and a classical style. Laurence Olivier also did it, for
instance in his productions of *Richard III* and *King Lear*; but the
French tradition is more strict than the English.

The production, the staging, the whole work of Vilar give
an impression of liberty, of freedom of style. How does he do it?

I have never seen him at rehearsals. His actors have sometimes
told me that they did not rehearse enough. His stage-director
has complained that the sets were not studied carefully enough.
In all this, there seems to be some carelessness, some looseness.
Every time I have seen a show, however, it has been in perfect
order, never mechanical, always meaningful and full of style –
with the occasional failures which are natural to any creative
artist. I was the more puzzled.

On the boat coming here I read a book by Vilar which has just
appeared. It is called *De la Tradition Théâtrale*.[1] I was at once
struck by the quality of the thinking, the concentration, the
density of that little book. It is never commonplace. It is lucid,
simple, and precise, never nebulous or philosophical, never
pretentious.

Vilar writes that one always tends to work on the stage too
soon and too long, giving too much time and care to what we
call placing, but which I believe the Americans call 'blocking'.
(Remember that his ideas assume a permanent company of
talented and well-trained actors.) 'One should,' he goes on to
say, 'not only give confidence to the actor but have confidence
in him. One never has enough confidence in his professional

1. L'Arche (Paris 1955)

intelligence and sensitivity. A third of the rehearsal time should be given to word rehearsals, what we call 'répéter à l'italienne'. When you put an actor on the stage too quickly, his physical reactions are too hastily provoked,' and Vilar writes, 'We must rehearse a lot'–in French: 'le corps au repos et le cul sur la chaise', which means – 'body at rest and bottom on a chair'. 'Cul' is a very good word.

'It's necessary,' he writes again, 'that the deep sensitivity of the actor, guided by the director, should be given time gradually to reach the right level.' And later, 'There is no part which has not to be characterised. There is no ready-made impersonation, there is no good acting without characterisation.' Very illuminating. And Vilar is not at all a man who caricatures anything. His style is very limpid. He also says, 'Placing (or blocking) and physical expression should be dealt with comparatively quickly by a truly professional actor, taking approximately fifteen rehearsals out of forty.' Is it not striking? I do not yet completely understand how he does it. And again, 'The director's art is one of suggestion, not imposition.' That we know. 'Above everything he must not be brutal. The actor's spirit is as important as the poet's. One does not reach somebody's mind by being brutal. It's on the mind of the actor rather than on his emotional quality that the good interpretation of a play depends.' And again, 'A director who does not know how to detach himself from his work during the last rehearsals, when he is most involved, is only a poor artisan, losing his sight, forgetting, the stupid fellow, that before anything else the theatre is "un jeu" where inspiration and childlike rapture are more important than sweat and fits of temper.'

I like the tendency which such an attitude reveals. I agree with it. Remember once more that it applies to a permanent and well trained company, where voice, body, and style are practised daily.

And all this is related to the idea of freedom which is unattainable without first-rate craftsmanship.

I believe that this freedom is the supreme goal of an artist who cannot be master of his art until he feels relaxed and natural. Classical art helps you on the difficult road to freedom. It helps you to acquire a lightness of touch and a concentration upon essentials. By picking you out of the mud of naturalism it raises you above your work.

I believe that a classical discipline equips you with sharper instruments with which to penetrate to the depths of realism.

To avoid the dangers inherent in classical practice one needs a good, broad, cultured background, and a long training. In my last lecture I shall say something about this training and my work at the Old Vic School.

TRAINING

FOR THE THEATRE

THE OLD VIC SCHOOL

THEATRE SCHOOLS seem to provoke many people, particularly theatre people, to hostility. They say that schools are dangerous: either because they are conventional and academic, perpetuating lifeless traditions, or because they are aggressively non-conforming and so become narrow, sectarian and theoretical, if not hysterical; and I will readily agree that geniuses and various romantic artists are better off without training in any school at all.

It is my hope, however, that schools of the kind I have promoted may contribute to solving some of the problems which the theatre of our time has got to face: having no definite style of its own, it wavers continually between a powerful classical tradition and the remarkable achievement of modern realism, which is still in the process of full evolution.

Like Louis Jouvet and Charles Dullin, I belonged to the school of Copeau. I have seen the work of Dullin's school, where Jean-Louis Barrault and Jean Vilar were trained. These two schools, Copeau's and Dullin's, were both of the non-conforming kind.

I have established and directed three non-conforming schools myself: The London Theatre Studio (1935-1939), the Old Vic

Theatre School (1946-1952), and l'École Supérieure d'Art Dramatique in Strasbourg which I opened in 1954. The two English schools have closed down but, at present, there are three schools in England which claim to follow, more or less closely, the basic principles of our teaching. The Strasbourg school, which was directed by my wife, Suria Magito, goes on. It suffers from fewer 'pressures' than the other two did. Strasbourg may be the capital of Europe but it is, all the same, a little out of the way.

I have chosen to speak to you about the Old Vic School because it bears a glorious name which has always had great popular appeal. It was also the most complete. It included among its staff some of the best people I had met in the English theatre. It had the exclusive service of men like my old friends George Devine and Glen Byam Shaw. We used to teach in the school, all three of us.

These three schools did not exist for their own sake. They had a common purpose. By training people in all branches of the theatre they sought to further the evolution of dramatic art. Concerning ourselves with all the means of expression which are characteristic of our time, we based our teaching on classical disciplines. Our aim, however, was always to enrich the modern theatre.

The practical purpose of the three schools was emphasised by the fact that the first one, which was called the London Theatre Studio (L.T.S.), attempted to establish a new company of actors. Its members took part in the principal productions I did before the war, both at the Old Vic and in the West End. Its most recent outcome has been the foundation, under George Devine, of the English Stage Company, which is modern both in repertory and attitude. It is also significant that Glen Byam

Shaw directed the Stratford Memorial Theatre for four years.

What were the main features of those three schools?

An 'ensemblier', according to the dictionary, is 'an artist who aims at unity of general effect'. We were 'ensembliers'. We set out to develop initiative, freedom, and a sense of responsibility in the individual, as long as he or she was ready and able to merge his personal qualities into the ensemble.

Our students were as limited as possible in numbers.

We never worked from or towards a system. Looking at the classics from a modern point of view we realised that artistic development is a very complex process. Every summer we revised and corrected our ways of working in close consultation with the staff and the more talented of the students who were leaving the school.

In order to create by degrees an alive and complete theatrical organisation, we found a way of making our staff and students realise the need to keep a creative attitude towards their work. First of all we encouraged invention and imagination. The school was always partly experimental; but to avoid conceit and extravagance we maintained that our chief practical purpose was wholly and above all to serve interpretation, and that in dealing with an important play it was healthy to consider the author as the only completely creative person: director, designer, and actor had to understand the author's intention and submit to it.

Our courses were divided between acting and technical courses: the acting courses were open to young students between the ages of seventeen and twenty-three. To this young group we tried to add another one, open to young actors already trained and in the profession. In the technical courses the age limit was much higher. We chose the modest description 'technical' so as to emphasise that we wanted concrete and even manual experience to come before the discussion of theoretical or æsthetic ideas.

We applied certain other basic principles in order that techniques should never be allowed to dominate and supersede invention and interfere with what is called truth. But we impressed on everybody that there was no possibility of expressing truth, especially truth to a theatrical style, without a strongly developed technique.

It has always been my experience that I do my best work in the theatre with stars working within a permanent company. In the school, however, it was not our purpose to obtain quick results and to create stars at the expense of the students' normal development. We were content to leave the cultivation of stars to hard work, good luck – and time.

Another of our main preoccupations was to provide the outgoing students with good professional opportunities, while at the same time refusing to consider ourselves as a machine through which students were obliged to pass if they wanted to emerge with the security of a job.

For the students' interpretative work, we liked to use whole plays or acts rather than isolated scenes, so that they would learn to consider their relationship with the other actors and the relative values of the different parts of the play. For detailed work on language and textual style, we used scenes from plays only in exceptional circumstances.

The students worked mostly in groups, each group being like a small company composed of boys and girls in equal numbers. Each group preserved its identity from year to year.

How long was the course? In England the beginners' acting course lasted for two years only. In Strasbourg I succeeded in organising the acting courses on a three-year basis – the grant given to the Strasbourg centre by the state and the local authority was much more considerable than in England. Experience has shown me that three years is the minimum time for a successful course in acting, mainly because of the lengthy nature of the work that has to be done on the voice and on the practice of language in various styles. May I mention that in Russia the length of the acting course is four years.

The technical courses were arranged on a one-year basis, the necessary time to train a good assistant stage-manager and to select from the course the few students to be admitted into an advanced course where would-be directors and designers worked in couples for one or two years more. They could then pursue their apprenticeship by becoming assistant instructors in the school, or stage-managers and stage-directors with the small companies which were formed from the best students after they had left the school. In Russia the length of study for direction or design is five years.

We planned continual contact between the various courses, which proved to be of great advantage to the development and unity of the school as a whole.

Every year, the training culminated in public performances. In London we used to give two completely different shows so that we could include as great a variety of styles as possible and give plenty of opportunities to the actors. We gave one-act plays or an act out of a full-length play. At the end of the second show we always gave an experimental work, often composed by a writer on our staff. We experimented a great deal with the relationship between music, the spoken word, and choral expression. In this way we gave works as varied as Offenbach's *La Vie Parisienne* and *Fortunio*, Kurt Weill's *Down in the Valley*; and an adaptation of the great Finnish legend *Kalevala* which

tells of the creation of the world as it is related in Finnish folk·
lore.

In London we gave these end-of-course shows for a fortnight
to paying audiences. The shows were run entirely by the students
from the box-office to the switch-board. They were directed
by the instructors with the help of their assistants. Costumes and
scenery were designed and made by the students of the Advanced
Technical course. Students in the first-year acting course took
part in the manual preparation of the show. We thought it would
not be beneath their dignity as artists to spend a short part of
their course doing something with their hands.

In Strasbourg we gave a single performance of a single show
in our theatre and then took it on tour for three weeks. Contact
with different audiences and a nightly change of location
familiarised young actors with theatrical conditions of the
hardest kind better than any other way I had devised.

In fact the students had already begun to make contact with
the public at the beginning of their second year when they were
called upon to transfer their feeling for truth and concentration
from private work in the class-rooms to public performances,
with or without the fourth wall.

I am afraid that I still have not reached the essential part of this
talk, the very nature of the training. If I am spending a lot of time
in the monotonous enumeration of the basic conditions on which
our work was established it is because these very conditions were
essential to bring about the happy freedom and the strong
discipline which are necessary for creative work in the
theatre.

The day's work began at nine o'clock and ended at five-thirty or six. On Saturdays it ended at one o'clock. During hectic rehearsal periods it continued in the evenings.

Until the end of the first term both sides were on trial. We and the students were trying each other out. After three months we were free to part from each other. From then on we were contracted to each other for the remainder of the course, though we reserved the opportunity of eliminating people at the end of each year for bad work or lack of discipline. Work outside the school was forbidden except with the authorisation of the director.

At the Old Vic School we received between four and five hundred applications a year. We took thirty-five students in the Acting course and twenty in the Technical course. Admission to the Acting course depended upon two auditions and an interview. Admission to the Technical courses depended, for would-be directors, on the written production of a single act from a classical play; for designers on the designing of a limited number of sets and costumes for a play of the same kind. Designers were also obliged to show all their past work in painting, drawing, sculpture, etc.

Scholarships: In France, tuition at the official schools is free: that is the rule. If necessary, maintenance grants are awarded by the state or the local authority. In England everybody pays a fee. At the Old Vic School, however, two-thirds of our students were on scholarships. The tuition fees were paid by the Education Authorities directly to the school, so that our budget, even if it did not break even, could be kept under control. Maintenance scholarships, the amount of which depended on the needs of the student's family, were paid directly to the students. It is important to point out that this excellent system was brought about in England by what has been called 'the silent revolution'.

THE OLD VIC, 1952
Electra. Set by Barbara Hepworth

Catherine Lacey as Clytemnestra and Lee Montague as **A** Slave

Peggy **A**shcroft as Electra, with Pauline Jameson as Chrysothemis, and Chorus

STRASBOURG, 1957: **A**bove, decor for *Tessa* (Jean Giraudoux), Act I.
Below, Students in a production of *The Mine* (Jean Claude Maney)

It changed completely the kind of students we received and consequently the spirit in the school. Owing to the popular appeal of the Old Vic we had young people coming to our school from all over the country, the Commonwealth, and the United States, very often with local accents, full of flavour, which we welcomed when they were not too strong.

A school of the kind we were trying to build cannot be a money-making proposition. It should be in a position to limit entry into an overcrowded profession to talented people. The Old Vic School received a grant of £4,500 a year. Though generous, this was inadequate.

I have reached at last the heart of my subject: the nature of the training itself, its purpose, its content, its ways and means.

Our purpose was twofold:

1. To bring reality to the interpretation of all theatrical styles, particularly the classical, and to achieve the greatest possible freedom in their practice.

2. To enlarge the actor's field of expression and to equip him in such a way that he could mime, sing, dance, perform acrobatic tricks, without specialising beyond the normal requirements of an actor.

In explaining how we tried to carry out this programme, I shall limit myself to the acting courses, omitting the Technical courses however important I consider them to be. In the same way, I shall have time to describe only the main aspects of the training, omitting many details of the curriculum.

On the very first day there began the technical training of the body (which is the first technical need of the actor), and very shortly afterwards of his voice: then a three weeks' rehearsal period of a big Shakespearian play, for instance, under the Head of the School. This latter was a rather nasty operation which we called 'the test'. It was like throwing a dog into the water, knowing it will never drown but in order to see how well it swims. At the end of three weeks members of the entire staff assembled in the school's theatre to watch 'the test'. This gave them an idea of each student's ability and behaviour on the stage. More important still, the Head of the School had the experience of three weeks' daily work with the new students. He had begun to get to know them and was now in a position to direct the ensuing discussions which took place at a general meeting of the staff. Notes taken by the teachers during the show were compared and it was possible to make decisions about the treatment of each student. Considered criticism and advice was then given to the students at a general meeting attended by them and the complete staff.

These critical sessions were among the most important features of the school. Full-length sessions were held at the end of every term, others of a more fragmentary character at half term. Members of the staff discovered the opinions and attitudes of other teachers towards the students, and the students themselves became accustomed to take criticism.

When test and criticism were over, the real training began with a few introductory explanations about the main lines it was going to follow. I avoided giving the students any theory about acting. We tried to guide them as they went along, so that they understood the purpose of each phase of their work and discovered slowly in their practical classes what it meant.

The training itself could be divided into three main parts – cultural, technical, and a central section which was concerned with improvisation and interpretation. This was the most important.

Each section was approached from a dramatic point of view. Academic attitudes were avoided. Behind all scholarly knowledge or intellectual considerations, there had to be the requirements of dramatic necessity.

In developing this concept, we tried to ensure that as far as possible every new technical or cultural development which we presented to the students should have a dramatic justification. For instance, study of the Commedia dell' Arte was justified when it was needed to support practical work in the improvisation of comic characters. Acrobatics came in when the students felt they needed greater physical freedom, better timing, or quicker control of their bodies.

To make certain that every part of the training would be inspired by dramatic necessity and that teachers would not be tempted to organise their departments into independent kingdoms, firstly certain classes and rehearsals were shared between teachers of different subjects-voice and movement, for example, and secondly the whole work of the school was divided into three main subjects with a responsible director at the head of each. Every teacher worked under one of these three divisions. In this way it was comparatively easy for the Head of the School to be in close touch with the three directors under him and so ensure practical liaison between them.

The three divisions were as follows:

A. *Movement* (the director of this division maintained particularly close touch with the work in improvisation). This included physical exercises for relaxation, physical alertness, control, and general strengthening; physical expression, exercises applied to a purpose or a mood conducive to dramatic expression: dancing beginning with folk dances of many countries and developing into period dances of varying styles; and fencing and acrobatics for poised relaxation leading to an agile sense and quick control of timing.

B. *Language* (the director of this division maintained a particularly close touch with the work in culture and interpretation). This included voice and its pitch, breathing and singing, diction and the correction of accents, choral speech and choral singing; reading and study of outstanding literary works, reading of examples of non-dramatic poetry and prose of different styles; and speech delivery of the great dramatic styles.

C. *Improvisation and Interpretation* (closely related to language and movement). This included silent and spoken improvisation (this will be explained later); the study in seminars and workshops of three main styles – classical tragedy, classical comedy, and realism in all its aspects; reading of plays of all styles; technique of rehearsals – experience in working through the successive phases of rehearsals under various directors; quick rehearsals of short scenes to develop various aspects of stage technique; lectures to provide an imaginative background to practical work on period texts, history of drama throughout the world, history of arts and customs as they are related to the great dramatic periods; study of the world's great novels (for example, Defoe, Dickens, Balzac, Dostoievsky, Tolstoy); study of period style in connection with the technical courses – exhibition of documents, wearing of costumes, handling of period properties (for example, swords, fans, snuff boxes), movement and dance related to the manners of the period, (for example, curtseys, bows, etc.); and music of the period.

The classes in style offered a central point of study and an opportuntity for common work in the whole school.

Make-up, the study of the world's great paintings, and visits to museums, were a part of this curriculum.

The study of cultural subjects was dealt with principally during the first year.

After this year various physical techniques were gradually dropped.

The study of language and vocal techniques, on the other hand, developed continually and especially during the final year.

I am now coming to the more interesting but more difficult material.

I have said that during the first year and up to the end of the first term in the second year, we placed the main emphasis upon improvisation. Immediately after the test the students, for a time, were kept away from working on dramatic texts, that is, plays. They did plenty of acting but it was of the improvised kind. The purpose of this was to give them an opportunity to discover for themselves, within themselves, what acting consists of. At the same time we put them in touch with non-dramatic texts of many different styles. We followed this plan in order that the students should have no opportunity to monkey with the text of a play until they knew something about the nature of a text and what it feels like to act. Meanwhile they soon began to learn how to rehearse, how to read a part aloud, and how to conduct themselves while a play is 'placed' or 'blocked'. That was all for the first year.

By the second year the students were supposed to have acquired basic experience in acting. Rehearsals could now go further, to the learning of lines, and the first running through of a play.

At the beginning of the second year the students' concentration would be extended to include their audience. They showed the results of their work in improvisation to a small audience and a little later they gave a show entirely comprised of poetry, music and singing, and dancing. At the end of the second year they gave, to a limited audience, their first show in the interpretation of style.

What do we mean by 'improvisation' and why do we attach such basic importance to it? Because we believe that on this bare and open field of action the young student, obliged to concentrate and to invent to the utmost, can experience the very fact of acting and can be led almost naturally and unconsciously to the mental and physical transposition required by style. In this branch of the work he acts for a year in complete silence without either the hindrance or the help of a written text.

Difficulties will arise when in due course the moment will have come to connect this silent improvisation with the interpretation of a text, to use the one for the animation of the other. We believe that an imaginative actor will never forget the kind of satisfaction he felt while improvising, if he has fully experienced it. With a little help he will be able to bring the benefit of this creative experience to the interpretation of a written text. We also believe that, in this early phase of his work, all the observations made about acting by the great masters of the past, including Stanislavski, with careful discrimination, can be put to use.

To begin with, the student in improvisation classes is dressed in his practice costume. He is as naked as possible. He has to conquer his self-consciousness. We can see his body at work with all its qualities and defects. He has no scenery. Nothing on the stage but a few stools if he wants them.

As the work progresses, he will move from an A B C made up of the representation of actions taken from his daily life like waking up, eating a meal, returning home, dressing and undressing, to moods that are complicated by external circumstances. He will soon begin to experience the need for concentration and observation; he will realise the importance of emotional memory. He will become aware of the use of space, of rhythm, of the continuity of action. At the same time the exercises he is given to do, however simple they may be, can never be 'naturalistic': the student must find out for himself and by himself how to represent on the stage those naturalistic actions which in real life would involve the handling of objects. So, progressing, he will go on to represent people of different crafts seen at their work in characteristic professional activities and then, move on to transformation – into circus types, into animals, even into the world of dreams. The next step will be the invention of a complete scenario with all the details of circumstance necessary to its complete realisation.

In all the work up till now the student has remained himself. There has been no attempt at characterisation, no concern with psychology.

This silent improvisation culminated in the use of masks, full-face masks of normal human size, simple and harmonious masks representing the four ages of man: the adolescent, the adult, mature middle-age and old-age. In getting the students to wear masks, we were not aiming at æsthetic results nor was it our intention to revive the art of mime. To us, a mask was a temporary instrument which we offered to the curiosity of the young actor, in the hope that it might help his concentration, strengthen his inner feelings, diminish his self-consciousness, and lead him to develop his powers of outward expression. A mask is a concrete object. When you put it on your face you receive from it a strong impulse which you have got to obey. But the mask is also an inanimate object which the personality of the actor will bring to life. As his inner feelings accumulate behind the mask, so the actor's face relaxes. His body, which is made more expressive by the very immobility of the mask, will be brought to action by the strength of inner feeling. Once the actor has acquired the elementary technique that is demanded by wearing a mask, he will begin to realise that masks dislike agitation, that they can only be animated by controlled, strong, and utterly simple actions which depend upon the richness of the inner life within the calm and balanced body of the performer. The mask absorbs the actor's personality from which it feeds. It warms his feelings and cools his head. It enables the actor to experience, in its most virulent form, the chemistry of acting: at the very moment when the actor's feelings are at their height, beneath the mask, the urgent necessity of controlling his physical actions compels him to detachment and lucidity. Submission to the lesson of the mask enables an actor of talent to discover a broad, inspired and objective style of acting. It is a good introduction to classical acting. It is a good preparatory school for tragedy and drama in its greatest styles. Scenarios using up to three actors were drawn from striking dramatic moments in classical tragedies or dramas. Further than this, silent improvisation cannot go.

Costumes were evolved by the actors, with the help of students from the Technical Courses, not from the decorative point of view, but to fulfil some strong dramatic purpose, to prolong or enhance his movements. In the same way, lightly constructed scenery was introduced, rostra, steps, screens, and essential pieces of furniture. Simple music also began to be used.

This phase of the work coincided with lively talks about the Greek, Chinese, and Japanese theatres, and tragedies from the seventeenth and eighteenth centuries.

Before the end of the first year the students were given experience of choral improvisation. The scenarios were based
on strong themes like war, exodus, crossing of the Red Sea,
floods, mine catastrophes, and so on. This was to enable the
entire group of twenty students to find a relationship with each
other in crowd scenes. Choral improvisation made use of sound:
the kind of meaningful but inarticulate sound by which the
mood of a crowd reveals itself, helped, if necessary, by noises
and music.

Comic improvisation fitted in at the beginning of the second
year. It was based on the invention of comic characters which
had to exist individually before they could meet in short
scenarios. The student was now given the opportunity to speak,
provided that the strength of his acting brought him to words,
but avoiding chatter or imposed and self-conscious nonsense.
We found that speech often sprang truthfully and genuinely
from comic characterisations. The students were allowed the
use of half-masks, noses, padding, disguises of all kinds, simple
scenery and props that were stimulating to act with.

Talks about the Commedia dell' Arte and Music Hall comedians were given in support of this work.

This led to the timing of gags, elements of acrobatics, all
the means and techniques of a comedian, together with singing
and the practice of musical instruments easy to handle, such as
guitar, flute, concertina, etc.

We have now reached the end of the first term of the second
year.

From then on everything until the conclusion of the training

[105]

was concentrated upon interpretation. You will have noticed that a good deal of practical work in interpretation had gone on from the very beginning of the course, but in a preparatory manner. The students had studied all kinds of texts, they had passed through the rehearsal stages of plays chosen from the three styles already mentioned, changing their text every five weeks. Their bodies had begun to be co-ordinated and many of the students in the course of their improvisations, had begun to discover some of the inner secrets of acting.

They had now to learn how to combine such discoveries as they had made with the speaking of difficult texts. They had to obtain control of their breathing, of the pitch of their voices, they had to experience how to handle dialogue in such a way that it was no longer an obstacle to their discovery of reality and truth in their acting. We found that a few of the students had a special gift for words, and their acting would blossom under the influence of written texts; but all of them needed to improve their sense of timing and the musical quality of their delivery. It is not enough for an actor to be heard: his voice has to translate the shape of the text and its tempo into meaningful sound and to produce the subtle modulations required by meaning and feeling.

In all this I may appear to insist too much upon form and technique. The truth is that to counterbalance the amount of imaginative experience acquired by the actors in their many different kinds of improvisation, the time had come for them to master form and style before they could regain their freedom of invention. Until then creative acting would remain an un-attainable paradise.

It was then that real talent and artistic temperament began to make themselves evident. Where they were lacking we had disordered emotions, strange inventiveness, and technical ex-hibitionism.

We were in pursuit of meaning and reality which can only be expressed by a strong vocal technique based on a fine appreciation of the nature and form of a text in all its aspects.

The training in interpretation reached its climax, and the young actor could be shown how to extract the meaning of a play as a whole: the meaning of the different sections of the play, the meaning of his own part in relation to the others. A young actor must understand and take into account the views of the director of the play, for it is on these views and on the kind of relationship established between the actor and his director, that the unity of the show will depend. It was then that the young actor, recalling his experiences in improvisation, had to attack the last phase of rehearsals, and finally, bring his character to life, both mentally and physically.

The field was now open. It was only complementary work that had to be accomplished. Everyone could now be aware that each play is not approached in the same manner. An actor has always got to start from the text; but in realistic style, the mean-ing often lies below the surface; and excessive work too early on a Chekhov text, for instance, might be extremely damaging. The contrary is true of plays of great style, such as those of Shakespeare, where the form of the verse and the words them-selves lead the actor to the reality of the characters.

All kinds of important exercises could now be practised with-out danger. For instance: exercises in speed for the sake of speed, the famous building of climaxes, quick ways to rehearse simple plays, and so on.

You must realise however, that real work on the complex problems of interpretation began as late as the second term of the second year. Do you understand now why three years are absolutely necessary? Do you understand why the Russians are using four years?

Do you also appreciate why a school of acting must recruit young people, adolescents? We aim at the complete professional development of this unique artist: an artist who is his own instrument; an artist who, apart from the necessary cleverness and even shrewdness which is required for the practice of any art, needs at the beginning of his career something of the naïve and open attitude which belongs naturally to children and tends to disappear after adolescence.

Of course it would be an excellent thing to add to this basic course an advanced one, composed of talented young actors who have already been trained elsewhere perhaps, or are already members of the theatrical profession.

A school of this kind should not exist in isolation. It should be related to an active theatre, the actors from which might find it profitable, from time to time, to return to school, to improve or develop one aspect or another of their talent. Then in the fourth year the school should have the opportunity of developing its own company so that what is original in the school's work can be shown properly to the public. Public appreciation and press criticisms might also help to kill at the roots the pretentiousness which is always liable to appear in young actors who feel they have received 'special' treatment.

One can conduct experiments in a school which cannot be attempted elsewhere. For that reason a good and daring school can be of great help to the theatre. The Old Vic School has left behind it groups of people who have continued to work together. In England as well as in the Commonwealth and certain foreign countries, these groups are doing inspired and successful work. This year in Strasbourg, a company created by former students has been touring the country with plays by Molière and Thornton Wilder. They are receiving considerable appreciation for the conviction and skill of their acting.

I have now come to the end of these talks about 'classical theatre' and 'modern realism'. I hope that they have helped to create an understanding of the interconnection of them both. I am aware that I have been speaking to you in a country that is producing a wealth of dramatists, directors, and designers of a talent that is having repercussions throughout the world.

American realism in the theatre is attracting interest and enjoying success for many reasons. American vitality is provocative: dramatists are demonstrating in their plays some of the troubles which disturb American society, and do not hesitate to expose, in their most intimate aspects, the exasperated emotions at work in the individual.

These revelations shock and rouse the old world, while at the same time they are welcomed for their boldness. They do not always convince, however, because they are often too personal. They fail in the last resort to give a true and significant picture of all the facets of American man.

The fact is that a similar anxiety is expressed by American dramatists themselves. In 1958 Arthur Miller in a lecture to *The New Dramatists* said: 'I believe we have arrived in America at the end of a period, because we are repeating ourselves season after season . . . There is one play after another in which a young person, usually male, usually sensitive, is driven either to self-destructive revolt or impotency by the insensitivity of his parents, usually the father . . . What is wrong is not the theme, but its failure to extend itself so as to open up ultimate causes . . .

The potential vision of these plays is not fulfilled, and their potential æsthetic size and perfection is left unrealised. And perhaps even more important, there is implicit in this cut-down vision a decay of nerve, a withering of power to grasp the whole world on the stage and shake it to its foundations as it is the historic job of drama to do . . . We refuse to reflect on our stage a level of objective awareness at least as great as exists commonly in our lives outside.'

But 'a level of objective awareness' is what you find in the classical theatre. And it is Arthur Miller again who said, 'I am not asking for anything new, but something as old as the Greek drama.'

I would like to hope that in the field of training for the stage, these lectures might make a contribution to the movement by which the American theatre, intent upon creating and building a dramatic tradition, is consciously in search of a style.

CPSIA information can be obtained
at www.ICGtesting.com
Printed in the USA
BVHW09s2046120918
527340BV00009B/86/P